SOCIAL ISSUES, JUSTICE AND STATUS

SAME-SEX ISSUES

SOCIAL ISSUES, JUSTICE AND STATUS

Additional books in this series can be found on Nova's website at:

https://www.novapublishers.com/catalog/index.php?cPath=23_29&seriesp=Social+Issues,+Justice+and+Status

Additional e-books in this series can be found on Nova's website at:

https://www.novapublishers.com/catalog/index.php?cPath=23_29&seriespe=Social+Issues,+Justice+and+Status

SOCIAL ISSUES, JUSTICE AND STATUS

SAME-SEX ISSUES

JASON V. ALBERTSON
EDITOR

Nova Science Publishers, Inc.
New York

For permission to use material from this book please contact us:
Telephone 631-231-7269; Fax 631-231-8175
Web Site: http://www.novapublishers.com

LIBRARY OF CONGRESS CATALOGING-IN-PUBLICATION DATA

Available upon request.
ISBN : 978-1-61668-220-0

Published by Nova Science Publishers, Inc. † New York

CONTENTS

PREFACE

In 2003, state courts began to address the constitutionality of state statutes limiting marriage to heterosexual couples. Currently, federal law does not recognize same-sex marriages. This book discusses the Defense of Marriage Act (DOMA), which prohibits federal recognition of same-sex marriages; the effect of same-sex marriage on social security benefits and pensions; same-sex adoptions; and examines homosexuals in the U.S. military.

Chapter 1 - With the 2004 legalization of same-sex marriage in Massachusetts,[1] many have questioned how the legalization of such marriages at the state level may affect the eligibility for and payment of federal Social Security benefits and private pensions. Social Security benefits are currently paid to the spouses of disabled, retired, or deceased workers entitled to Social Security. However, under current law, same-sex spouses are not eligible for Social Security benefits because they are unable to meet the gender- based definitions of "wife" and "husband" in the Social Security Act and the gender-based definition of "marriage" established by the Defense of Marriage Act. Federal employee pensions and private-sector pensions regulated by the Employee Retirement Income Security Act (ERISA) are required to provide certain benefits to the spouse of a participant in the event of the participant's death. Under the Defense of Marriage Act, both federal pensions and private-sector pensions regulated by ERISA are required to define a spouse only as "a person of the opposite sex who is a husband or a wife."

Chapter 2 - State laws concerning the eligibility of homosexuals to adopt vary. Some states statutorily prohibit such action, while others are silent on the issue, leaving interpretation to the courts. This chapter summarizes state laws concerning non-relative adoption by homosexual individuals and couples. The report will be updated as developments warrant.

Chapter 3 - In 2003, state courts began to address the constitutionality of state statutes limiting marriage to heterosexual couples. Massachusetts became the first state to legalize marriage between same-sex couples on May 17, 2004, after the state's highest court held that denying gay and lesbian couples the right to marry violated the state's constitution. Subsequently, state courts in New Jersey, California, Connecticut, and Iowa reached similar conclusions. In addition, the California, Connecticut and Iowa Supreme Courts found that domestic partnership/civil union laws are not the constitutional equivalent of civil marriage. However, in New Jersey, the court left open the option for the state legislature to provide a parallel statutory structure (i.e., civil unions) in which same-sex couples would enjoy the same rights, privileges, and burdens as married opposite-sex couples.

While the aforementioned states legalized same-sex marriages judicially, Vermont became the first state to legalize same-sex marriages legislatively on April 7, 2009. State legislators garnered a sufficient number of votes to override the governor's veto. Maine and New Hampshire subsequently legalized same-sex marriages.

In California, voters approved a constitutional amendment limiting the validity and recognition of "marriages" to heterosexual couples. This constitutional amendment is intended to overrule the California Supreme Court's decision. On May 26, 2009, the California Supreme Court upheld the constitutional amendment. However, the court found that the amendment applies only prospectively, and does not affect the continued validity of the estimated 18,000 same-sex marriages that occurred prior to the amendment's passage.

Currently, federal law does not recognize same-sex marriages. This chapter discusses the Defense of Marriage Act (DOMA), P.L. 104-199, which prohibits federal recognition of same-sex marriages and allows individual states to refuse to recognize such marriages performed in other states, and discusses the potential legal challenges to DOMA. It reviews legal principles applied to determine the validity of a marriage contracted in another state, surveys the various approaches employed by states to prevent same-sex marriage, and examines House and Senate resolutions introduced in previous Congresses proposing a constitutional amendment and limiting federal courts' jurisdiction to hear or determine any question pertaining to the interpretation of the DOMA.

Chapter 4 - In 1993, new laws and regulations pertaining to homosexuals and U.S. military service came into effect reflecting a compromise in policy. This compromise, colloquially referred to as "don't ask, don't tell," holds that the presence in the armed forces of persons who demonstrate a propensity or intent to engage in homosexual acts would create an unacceptable risk to the high standards of morale, good order and discipline, and unit cohesion which are the essence of military capability. Service members are not to be asked about nor allowed to discuss their homosexuality. This compromise notwithstanding, the issue has remained politically contentious.

Prior to the 1993 compromise, the number of individuals discharged for homosexuality was generally declining. Since that time, the number of discharges for homosexual conduct has generally increased until recently.

Constitutional challenges to the former and current military policies regarding homosexuals followed in the wake of the new 1993 laws and regulations. Based on the U.S. Supreme Court ruling in *Bowers v. Hardwick* that there is no fundamental right to engage in consensual homosexual sodomy, the courts have uniformly held that the military may discharge a service member for overt homosexual conduct. However, the legal picture was complicated by the Court's 2003 decision in *Lawrence v. Texas* which overruled *Bowers* by declaring unconstitutional a Texas law that prohibited sexual acts between same sex couples. In addition, unsettled legal questions remain as to whether a discharge based solely on a statement that a service member is homosexual transgresses constitutional limits. Meanwhile, efforts to allow individuals of the same sex to marry legally appear unlikely to affect the Department of Defense (DOD) policy in the near term, since such individuals are barred from serving in the military, although court challenges are possible.

In addition, many academic institutions have enacted rules that protect homosexuals from discrimination on campus. As a result, colleges, universities, and even high schools have sought to bar military recruiters from their campuses and/or to eliminate Reserve Officer Training Corps (ROTC) programs on campus because of the DOD policy on homosexuals in the military. At the same time, legislation has been enacted that bars giving federal funds to campuses that block access for military recruiters. On March 6, 2006, the Supreme Court reversed a federal appeals court ruling in *Rumsfeld v. Forum for Academic and Institutional Rights (FAIR),* and upheld the constitutionality of the Solomon Amendment, which prohibits certain federal funding to higher educational institutions that deny access by military recruiters to their students equal to that provided to other employers.

In recent years, several members of Congress have expressed interest in amending "don't ask, don't tell." At least one bill that would repeal the law and replace it with a policy of nondiscrimination on the basis of sexual orientation—H.R. 1 283—has been introduced in the 111th Congress.

In: Same-Sex Issues
Editors: Jason V. Albertson
ISBN: 978-1-61668-220-0

Chapter 1

THE EFFECT OF STATE-LEGALIZED SAME-SEX MARRIAGE ON SOCIAL SECURITY BENEFITS AND PENSIONS

Laura Haltzel and Patrick Purcell
Income Security, Domestic Social Policy Division

SUMMARY

With the 2004 legalization of same-sex marriage in Massachusetts,[1] many have questioned how the legalization of such marriages at the state level may affect the eligibility for and payment of federal Social Security benefits and private pensions. Social Security benefits are currently paid to the spouses of disabled, retired, or deceased workers entitled to Social Security. However, under current law, same-sex spouses are not eligible for Social Security benefits because they are unable to meet the gender- based definitions of "wife" and "husband" in the Social Security Act and the gender- based definition of "marriage" established by the Defense of Marriage Act. Federal employee pensions and private-sector pensions regulated by the Employee Retirement Income Security Act (ERISA) are required to provide certain benefits to the spouse of a participant in the event of the participant's death. Under the Defense of Marriage Act, both federal pensions and private-sector pensions regulated by ERISA are required to define a spouse only as "a person of the opposite sex who is a husband or a wife."

SOCIAL SECURITY

Generally, Social Security benefits are payable to the spouses of retired, disabled, or deceased workers covered by Social Security. Spousal benefits are intended for individuals who are financially dependent on spouses who work in Social Security- covered positions. The spousal benefit is equal to 50% of the retired or disabled worker's benefit and 100% of the deceased worker's benefit.

The Social Security Act generally defers the determination of whether a marriage is valid for the purpose of qualifying for spousal or survivor benefits to the state of residence of the worker.[2] One might interpret this deferral to the state-level definition of marriage as permitting a same-sex spouse to be eligible for Social Security spousal benefits if such marriages are legal in that state. However, the definitions of "wife" and "husband" in the Social Security Act rely on gender-specific pronouns. The Social Security Act defines a person as the "wife" of an individual if *she* either (1) is the mother of *his* son or daughter; (2) is married to *him* for at least a year before filing for benefits; or (3) in the month prior to *her* marriage to *him* was entitled to (or if she had applied and been old enough would have been entitled to) Social Security benefits as a spouse, widow, parent, or disabled child.[3] Similarly, the act defines a person as the "husband" of an individual if *he* either (1) is the father of *her* son or daughter; (2) is married to *her* for at least a year before filing for benefits; or (3) in the month prior to *his* marriage to *her* was entitled to Social Security benefits as a spouse, widow, parent or disabled child.[4] The Social Security Administration (SSA) interprets this use of gender-specific pronouns as an indication that Congress did not intend same-sex spouses or survivors to be eligible for Social Security benefits.[5] Regardless of the SSA position, the Defense of Marriage Act of 1996 (DOMA, P.L. 104-199) established the legal definition of "marriage" as only a legal union between one man and one woman as husband and wife, and defined a "spouse" as only a person of the opposite sex who is a husband or wife when determining the meaning of any act of Congress, ruling, regulation, or interpretation by federal agencies. The SSA must use this federal definition of marriage when interpreting the Social Security Act. Therefore, the legalization of same-sex marriage at the state level has no effect in determining the validity of marriage for Social Security purposes.[6]

Federal Employee Pensions

Federal employees with permanent appointments are eligible for retirement and disability benefits under either the Civil Service Retirement System (CSRS) or the Federal Employees Retirement System (FERS). All federal employees initially hired into permanent federal employment on or after January 1, 1984 are covered by FERS. Employees hired before January 1, 1984, are covered by CSRS unless they chose to switch to FERS during open seasons held in 1987 and 1998. Both FERS and CSRS provide survivor benefits for the spouse and dependent children of a deceased federal employee or retiree.[7] Title 5 of the U.S. Code, which governs benefits under CSRS and FERS, defines the term "spouse"without reference to the individual's gender. Title 5 does not define the word "marriage"; however, the *Code of Federal Regulations* defines "marriage" for purposes of determining eligibility for federal retirement benefits under Title 5 as "a marriage recognized in law or equity under the whole law of the jurisdiction with the most significant interest in the marital status of the employee, member, or retiree unless the law of that jurisdiction is contrary to the public policy of the United States."[8]

Because federal employee retirement benefits under both CSRS and FERS are subject to the statutory interpretation required by the Defense of Marriage Act, in determining eligibility for survivor or dependant benefits under CSRS or FERS, "the word 'spouse' refers only to a person of the opposite sex who is a husband or a wife."[9]

Although a federal employee cannot name a domestic partner as his or her surviving beneficiary under either FERS or CSRS, an employee who is applying for a non-disability retirement can elect an Insurable Interest Annuity (IIA). Only one person may be named as the beneficiary of the IIA, and the election must be made at the time of retirement. The person named as the beneficiary must be someone who is financially dependent on the employee and the employee must establish, through one or more affidavits from other people, the reasons why the beneficiary might reasonably expect to suffer loss of financial support as a result of the employee's death. The cost of an IIA can range from a 10% reduction in the employee's retirement annuity if the beneficiary is 10 years younger than the employee to a 40% reduction if the beneficiary is 30 or more years younger.

Under both FERS and CSRS, an employee may designate a domestic partner as his or her beneficiary for a lump-sum refund of retirement contributions to the retirement system. However, if anyone qualifies to receive survivor annuity benefits by law (such as a spouse or dependent child), retirement contributions cannot be refunded. A federal employee also can name a domestic partner as the beneficiary under the Thrift Savings Plan (TSP), and he or she can designate a domestic partner as the beneficiary under the Federal Employee Group Life Insurance (FEGLI) program.

PRIVATE-SECTOR PENSIONS

Employers in the private sector are not required to offer pension benefits, but those that do must comply with the Employee Retirement Income Security Act (ERISA, P.L. 93-406). Section 5 14(a) of ERISA provides that the law preempts all state laws relating to employee benefits that are covered by ERISA.[10] Employer-sponsored pension plans also must comply with the relevant provisions of the Internal Revenue Code (IRC) in order to qualify for the preferential tax treatment granted to qualified pension plans.[11] Under the IRC, a tax-qualified defined-benefit pension must provide a married participant with a qualified pre-retirement survivor annuity (QPSA) while working and a qualified joint and survivor annuity (QJSA) at retirement.[12] A married participant must obtain his or her spouse's written approval either to waive a QJSA or a QPSA or to use a pension benefit as security for a loan.[13] Defined-contribution plans, such as §401(k) plans, pay the account balance to the designated beneficiary if the participant dies. The employee's spouse is the automatic beneficiary of the employee's account upon his or her death unless the employee has designated another beneficiary. The spouse's consent is not required in order for a participant in a defined-contribution plan to designate another beneficiary or beneficiaries in the event of the participant's death.

In administering federal income taxes, the Internal Revenue Service (IRS) has historically maintained that an individual is considered to be a "spouse" if the applicable state law recognizes the relationship as a marriage. If, for example, state law recognizes common-law marriages as legal, an employer in that state will be required to recognize an employee's common-law spouse as his or her legal spouse and IRS will recognize the marriage as valid. The IRS has never recognized same-sex marriages for income tax purposes, and the Defense of Marriage Act prohibits it from doing so, regardless of any state law. Moreover, while an employer may voluntarily extend benefits to the same-sex domestic partners of its employees, the DOMA supersedes state or local laws that would require an employer to recognize a same-sex partner as an employee's spouse for purposes of administering employer-sponsored retirement plans.

As noted above, tax-qualified pension plans are required to provide a qualified jointand-survivor annuity to a married participant and spouse, unless both spouses decline the QJSA in writing. Because DOMA prohibits employers from recognizing same-sex marriage for purposes of administering pension plans, a plan cannot require a participant with a same-sex partner to take a QJSA as the normal form of benefit, even if state law recognizes the same-sex partner as a spouse, because federal law (DOMA) prohibits federally regulated plans from recognizing a same-sex partner as a spouse.[14]

DOMA provides that, in interpreting any federal statute, ruling, or regulation — including, for example, ERISA and the Internal Revenue Code — a spouse can only be a person of the opposite sex who is a husband or wife. Consequently, a pension plan cannot be required to recognize a same-sex spouse even if same-sex marriages are permitted under state law.[15] Some benefits specialists have suggested that because Section 514(a) of ERISA preempts state laws that relate to employee benefits covered by ERISA, ERISA would therefore preempt any state law requiring the plan to recognize same-sex marriage for purposes of administering pension benefits. However, whether ERISA alone would preempt state laws recognizing same-sex marriage is irrelevant because DOMA prohibits recognition of same-sex spouses in the interpretation and application of federal law.

Bills in the 110th Congress

Several bills have been introduced in the 110th Congress to address the issue of same-sex marriage. H.J.Res. 22 is a proposed constitutional amendment that would amend the United States Constitution to state that "marriage in the United States shall consist only of a legal union of one man and one woman" and that "no State shall be required to give effect to any public act, record, or judicial proceeding of any other State concerning a union between persons of the same sex that is treated as a marriage, or as having the legal incidents of marriage, under the laws of such other State."

H.R. 107 would define marriage for all legal purposes in the District of Columbia to consist of the union of one man and one woman. H.R. 724 would amend Title 28 of the United State Code to limit federal court jurisdiction over questions under DOMA.

S. 2521, the Domestic Partner Benefits and Obligations Act, would extend benefits to domestic partners of federal employees. Under the act, same-sex domestic partners of federal employees would be eligible for benefits under the Federal Employees' Health Benefits Program, long-term care insurance, and the Federal Employees' Retirement System under the same conditions as spouses of married employees.

End Notes

[1] In *Goodridge v. Department of Public Health*, the Massachusetts Supreme Judicial Court ruled that under the state constitution, same-sex couples have the right to marry. The court later advised the state legislature that civil unions would not meet the requirements of the *Goodridge* decision.

[2] 42 U.S.C.416(h).

[3] 42 U.S.C. 4 16(b).

[4] 42 U.S.C. 416(f).

[5] See Section GN 00305.005 of the SSA *Program Operations Manual System*, Paragraph B(5). This manual is used by SSA employees to administer federal law, regulations, and rulings.

[6] Some have challenged the constitutionality of the Defense of Marriage Act. This legal question is beyond the scope of this chapter. Readers interested in this issue should refer to CRS Report RL3 1994, *Same-Sex Marriages: Legal Issues*, by Alison M. Smith.

[7] See CRS Report RS2 1029, *Survivor Benefits for Families of Civilian Federal Employees and Retirees*, by Patrick Purcell.

[8] See 5 C.F.R. §831.603 and 5 C.F.R. §843.102.

[9] 1 U.S.C. §7.

[10] 29 U.S.C. §1144(a).

[11] Employer contributions to a qualified plan are a tax-deductible expense for the employer and are not included in the income of the employee.

[12] 26 U.S.C. §401(a)(11) and §401(a)(17).

[13] 26 U.S.C. §417(a) and Treasury Regulation §1.401(a)-20, A-24, respectively.

[14] Some analysts have suggested that because the IRC does not restrict who is considered to be a "survivor," a plan could require a same-sex partner's consent to name anyone else as the recipient of a death benefit or contingent annuity, even though the plan could not require a retiring participant with a same-sex partner to take a qualifying joint and survivor annuity instead of a single-life annuity. See Neal S. Schelberg and Carrie L. Mitnick, "Same-Sex Marriage: Implications for Employee Benefit Plans,"*Employee Benefits Journal*, vol. 29, no. 2, June 2004.

[15] For example, because DOMA prohibits recognition of same-sex marriage, an employer could not be required to comply with a qualified domestic relations order (QDRO) from a state court in which a spouse in a same-sex marriage was named as an alternate payee of a pension benefit.

In: Same-Sex Issues
Editors: Jason V. Albertson
ISBN: 978-1-61668-220-0

Chapter 2

SAME-SEX ADOPTIONS

Alison M. Smith

SUMMARY

State laws concerning the eligibility of homosexuals to adopt vary. Some states statutorily prohibit such action, while others are silent on the issue, leaving interpretation to the courts. This chapter summarizes state laws concerning non-relative adoption by homosexual individuals and couples. The report will be updated as developments warrant.

Consistent with other areas of family law, adoption statutes are promulgated by state legislatures in accordance with public policy considerations that often include providing for the best interests of the child, achieving finality in the placement of children and promoting stability in family relations. Thus, individual states have different statutes regarding non-relative adoption by homosexual individuals and couples.[1]

Most states currently permit an individual gay or lesbian adult to adopt a minor child subject, as in any adoption, to a finding by a judge, that adoption by that individual is in the child's best interest.[2] State statutes concerning the eligibility of homosexuals to adopt range from Florida's statutory prohibition[3] on homosexual individuals adopting to Mississippi's statute barring adoption by same-sex couples[4] to Utah's prohibition on cohabitating unmarried couples, heterosexual or homosexual, from adopting.[5] Many state statutes are silent on the issue, leaving the subject open to interpretation by courts.[6] For example, the Ohio Supreme Court permitted the adoption of a "special needs" child by a homosexual, stating that there is a need to review adoption applications on a case-by-case basis without exacting any clear-cut rules regarding homosexual applicants.[7] Similarly, a New Jersey court allowed a homosexual couple to adopt a special needs child whom they fostered for approximately two years.[8]

On January 28, 2004, the U.S. Court of Appeals for the 11th Circuit affirmed a lower court decision[9] upholding a Florida statute banning adoption by homosexual individuals. In *Lofton v. Sec. of the Dept. of Children and Family Services*,[10] the court found that a Florida statute denying homosexuals the right to adopt does not violate the constitutional guarantees of equal protection or due process under the 14th Amendment of the U.S. Constitution.[11] In addressing the plaintiffs' due process claim, the court emphasized that there is no fundamental right to adopt, nor a fundamental right to be adopted as adoption is a privilege created by statute and not by common law.[12] Thus, the court reasoned there can be no fundamental right to apply for adoption.[13] As such, the liberty interest biological parents enjoy in raising their children without state interference could not be extended to a foster parent or guardian based merely on the existence of strong emotional ties between the foster parent or guardian and the child.[14]

Moreover, the court rejected plaintiffs' argument that the Supreme Court's decision in *Lawrence v. Texas*,[15] identified an unarticulated fundamental right to private sexual intimacy. The court stated that it was "hesitant to infer a new fundamental liberty interest from an opinion whose language and reasoning are inconsistent with standard fundamental-rights analysis."[16] The court noted the absence of "two primary features" of fundamental-rights analysis in the *Lawrence* decision.[17] First, the court stated that the *Lawrence* opinion contained "virtually no inquiry into the question of whether the petitioners' asserted right is one of those fundamental rights and liberties which are, objectively, deeply rooted in this Nation's history and tradition and implicit in the concept of ordered liberty, such that neither liberty nor justice would exist if they were sacrificed."[18] Second, the court noted that the *Lawrence* opinion "notably never provides the careful description of the asserted fundamental liberty interest" that is to accompany fundamental-rights analysis.[19]

Moreover, the court found that the holding of *Lawrence* did not control in the adoption context as *Lawrence* was limited to consenting adults and a criminal prohibition. The court reiterated that the relevant state action was not a criminal prohibition, but a grant of a statutory privilege. In addition the court stated that "the asserted liberty interest is not the negative right to engage in private conduct without facing criminal sanctions, but the affirmative right to receive official and public recognition."[20] Therefore, the court concluded that the *Lawrence* decision could not be extrapolated to create a right to adopt for homosexual persons.[21]

Addressing the equal protection argument, the court rejected the plaintiffs' assertion that the court should apply strict scrutiny in analyzing the statute. The court noted that as Florida's adoption statute burdens no fundamental right nor suspect class, the appropriate standard of review was rational basis. The court found that Florida has a legitimate interest in encouraging a stable and nurturing environment for the education and socialization of its adopted children.[22] In addition, the court reasoned that the state has a legitimate interest in encouraging an optimal family structure by seeking to place adoptive children in homes that have both a mother and father.[23]

The court rejected appellants' argument that the statute was not rationally related to this interest by noting that "it is entirely irrelevant for constitutional purposes whether the conceived reason for the challenged distinction actually motivated the legislature." Moreover, the court stated that neither the fact that a statutory classification may be overinclusive or underinclusive nor the fact that the generalization underlying the classification is subject to exception renders such a classification irrational, for purposes of equal protection.[24] Instead, the court stated that the question "is whether the Florida legislature could have reasonably believed that prohibiting adoption into homosexual environments would further its interest in placing adoptive children in homes that will provide them with optimal developmental conditions." The court found that there are plausible rational reasons for the disparate treatment of homosexuals under Florida adoption law.

Finally, the court noted that "any argument that the Florida legislature was misguided in its decision is one of legislative policy, not constitutional law. The legislature is the proper forum for this debate, and we do not sit as a superlegislature 'to award by judicial decree what was not achievable by political consensus.'"

On January 10, 2005, the United States Supreme Court, without comment, declined to hear the case.[25]

End Notes

[1] The related issue of second-parent adoption is beyond the scope of this chapter. A second-parent adoption is a legal procedure which allows a same-sex co-parent to adopt his or her partner's child.

[2] Numerous factors converge and influence this standard, including the home environment, stability of the parents, the time a parent and child spend together, the quality of the relationship between parent and child, sexual conduct and criminal background of the parents, as well as other factors the court deems appropriate. See 2 Am. Jur. 2d Adoption § 137. Florida is currently the only state which prohibits homosexual individuals from adopting. Fla. Stat. Ann. 63.042.

[3] Fla. Stat. Ann. 63.042 (3). On January 28, 2004, the 11th Circuit Court of Appeals found that the statute does not violate the Equal Protection or Due Process Clauses of the Fourteenth Amendment. *Lofton v. Sec. of the Dept. of Children and Family Services*, 358 F.3d 804, 816 (11th Cir. 2004). However, on August 29, 2008, a state court found this statute facially invalid under the state's constitution. Specifically, the court held that the statutory ban violated constitutional provisions pertaining to adoption, prohibiting bills of attainder and separation of powers. *In re Adoption of John Doe*, 2008 WL 5070056 (Fla. Cir. Ct. Aug. 29, 2008).

[4] Miss Ann. Code § 93-17-3(5).

[5] Utah Stat. § 78B-6-117. The statute does not expressly prohibit adoption by single people, nor does it ban same-sex couples from adopting from private agencies. On November 4, 2008, voters in Arkansas approved a similar citizen- initiated statute prohibiting unmarried sexual partners (both opposite-sex and same-sex couples) from adopting or serving as foster parents.In a related issue, Oklahoma passed the Oklahoma Adoption Invalidation Law (OK. Stat. Tit. 10 § 7502-1.4(A)), which prohibits the state from acknowledging adoptions by same-sex couples from other jurisdictions. The 10th Circuit Court of Appeals affirmed a lower court's ruling that the law, by its refusal to recognize and give effect to a valid judgment from another court of competent jurisdiction, which established their status as parents of their respective children, violates the Full Faith and Credit Clause of the United States Constitution. *Finstuen v. Crutcher,* 496 F.3d 1139 (10th Cir. 2007).

[6] See, e.g., *In re Lace*, 516 N.W.2d 678, 686 (Wis. 1994) (barring adoption of mother's daughter by mother's female partner because statutory scheme "balances society's interest in promoting stable, legally recognized families with its interests in promoting the best interests of the children involved.") see also, e.g., *Adoption of Tammy,* 619 N.E.2d 315 (Mass. 1993) (holding that Massachusetts law did not preclude same-sex cohabitants from jointly adopting a child); *Adoptions of B.L. V.B & E.L. V.B.*, 628 A.2d 1271 (Vt. 1993) (holding Vermont law does not require the termination of a natural mother's parental rights if her children are adopted by a person to whom she is not married, if it is in the best interests of the children).

[7] *In re Adoption of Charles B.*, 552 N.E. 2d 884 (Ohio 1990). "Special needs" child refers to the fact that Charles B. suffered from leukemia, possible brain damage from fetal alcohol syndrome, a low I.Q., and a speech impediment. His natural family abused him and he lived in four different foster homes. These factors led the court to believe that Charles B. would be better off with his adoptive parent, a homosexual, instead of in an institution or moving from foster home to foster home. *Id.*

[8] See, Joyce F. Sims, "*Homosexuals Battling the Barriers of Mainstream Adoption-And Winning,*" 23 T. Marshall L. Rev. 551, 581 (1998). Subsequently, the parties entered into an agreement in which gay and unmarried couples will be measured by the same adoption standards as married couples. Furthermore, no couple could be barred from adoption based on their sexual orientation or marital status.

[9] *Lofton v. Kearney*, 157 F.Supp.2d 1372 (S.D. Fla. 2001).

[10] 358 F.3d 804 (11th Cir. 2004). This marked the first time a federal appellate court addressed the constitutionality of banning adoption by homosexual individuals.

[11] *Id.*

[12] *Id.* at 809-811.

[13] *Id.*

[14] *Id.*

[15] 539 U.S. 558 (2003) (holding that substantive due process does not permit a state to impose a criminal prohibition on private consensual homosexual conduct between adults). For a legal analysis of this decision, refer to CRS Report RL3 1681, *Homosexuality and the Constitution: A Legal Analysis of the Supreme Court Ruling in Lawrence v. Texas*, by Jody Feder.

[16] *Lofton v. Sec. of the Dept. of Children and Family Services*, 358 F.3d 804, 816 (11th Cir. 2004).

[17] *Id.*

[18] *Id.*

[19] *Id.*

[20] *Id.* at 817.

[21] *Id.*

[22] *Id.* at 818.

[23] *Id.*

[24] *Id.* at 819.

[25] 358 F.3d 804 (11th Cir. 2004), pet. for cert.denied 73 U.S.L.W. 3399.

In: Same-Sex Issues
Editors: Jason V. Albertson

ISBN: 978-1-61668-220-0

Chapter 3

SAME-SEX MARRIAGES: LEGAL ISSUES

Alison M. Smith

SUMMARY

In 2003, state courts began to address the constitutionality of state statutes limiting marriage to heterosexual couples. Massachusetts became the first state to legalize marriage between same-sex couples on May 17, 2004, after the state's highest court held that denying gay and lesbian couples the right to marry violated the state's constitution. Subsequently, state courts in New Jersey, California, Connecticut, and Iowa reached similar conclusions. In addition, the California, Connecticut and Iowa Supreme Courts found that domestic partnership/civil union laws are not the constitutional equivalent of civil marriage. However, in New Jersey, the court left open the option for the state legislature to provide a parallel statutory structure (i.e., civil unions) in which same-sex couples would enjoy the same rights, privileges, and burdens as married opposite-sex couples.

While the aforementioned states legalized same-sex marriages judicially, Vermont became the first state to legalize same-sex marriages legislatively on April 7, 2009. State legislators garnered a sufficient number of votes to override the governor's veto. Maine and New Hampshire subsequently legalized same-sex marriages.

In California, voters approved a constitutional amendment limiting the validity and recognition of "marriages" to heterosexual couples. This constitutional amendment is intended to overrule the California Supreme Court's decision. On May 26, 2009, the California Supreme Court upheld the constitutional amendment. However, the court found that the amendment applies only prospectively, and does not affect the continued validity of the estimated 18,000 same-sex marriages that occurred prior to the amendment's passage.

Currently, federal law does not recognize same-sex marriages. This chapter discusses the Defense of Marriage Act (DOMA), P.L. 104-199, which prohibits federal recognition of same-sex marriages and allows individual states to refuse to recognize such marriages performed in other states, and discusses the potential legal challenges to DOMA. It reviews legal principles applied to determine the validity of a marriage contracted in another state, surveys the various approaches employed by states to prevent same-sex marriage, and examines House and Senate resolutions introduced in previous Congresses proposing a constitutional amendment and limiting federal courts' jurisdiction to hear or determine any question pertaining to the interpretation of the DOMA.

INTRODUCTION

Massachusetts became the first state to legalize marriage between same-sex couples on May 17, 2004, as a result of a November 2003 decision by the state's highest court that denying gay and lesbian couples the right to marry violated the state's constitution.[1] Similarly, state supreme courts in New Jersey,[2] California,[3] Connecticut,[4] and Iowa[5] found that denying same-sex couples the right to marry violated their state constitutions. In addition, the California, Connecticut, and Iowa courts found that parallel statutory structures, including domestic partnerships and/or civil unions, were not the constitutional equivalent of civil marriage. However, in New Jersey, the court left open the option for the state legislature to provide a parallel statutory structure which would allow same-sex couples to enjoy the same rights, privileges, and burdens as married opposite-sex couples.[6] While the aforementioned states legalized same-sex marriages judicially, on April 7, 2009, Vermont became the first state to legalize same-sex marriages legislatively. State legislators garnered a sufficient number of votes to override the governor's veto. Similarly, governors in Maine and New Hampshire signed bills legalizing same-sex marriages.

Currently federal law does not recognize, nor does any state law other than Vermont, Maine, and New Hampshire affirmatively allow gay or lesbian couples to marry. On the federal level, Congress enacted the Defense of Marriage Act (DOMA) to prohibit recognition of same-sex marriages for purposes of federal enactments. States, such as Alabama,[7] Alaska, Arkansas,[8] Arizona,[9] California,[10] Colorado,[11] Florida,[12] Georgia,[13] Hawaii, Idaho,[14] Kansas,[15] Kentucky,[16] Louisiana,[17] Michigan,[18] Mississippi,[19] Missouri,[20] Montana,[21] Nebraska,[22] Nevada, North Dakota,[23] Ohio,[24] Oklahoma,[25] Oregon,[26] South Carolina,[27] South Dakota,[28] Tennessee,[29] Texas,[30] Utah, Virginia,[31] and Wisconsin[32] have enacted state constitutional amendments limiting marriage to one man and one woman. Seventeen other states have enacted statutes limiting marriage in some manner.[33] **Table 1** summarizes these various approaches.

DEFENSE OF MARRIAGE ACT (DOMA)[34]

In 1996, Congress approved the DOMA "[t]o define and protect the institution of marriage." It allows all states, territories, possessions, and Indian tribes to refuse to recognize an act of any other jurisdiction that designates a relationship between individuals of the same sex as a marriage. In part, DOMA states:

> No State, territory, or possession of the United States, or Indian tribe, shall be required to give effect to any public act, record, or judicial proceeding of any other State, territory, possession, or tribe respecting a relationship between persons of the same sex that is treated as a marriage under the laws of such other State, territory, possession, or tribe, or a right or claim arising from such relationship.[35]

Furthermore, DOMA goes on to declare that the terms "marriage" and "spouse," as used in federal enactments, exclude same-sex marriage.

> In determining the meaning of any Act of Congress, or of any ruling, regulation, or interpretation of the various administrative bureaus and agencies of the United States, **the word 'marriage' means only a legal union** between one man and one woman as husband and wife, and the word **'spouse' refers only to a person of the opposite sex** who is a husband or a wife.[36]

POTENTIAL CONSTITUTIONAL CHALLENGES TO DOMA[37]

Full Faith and Credit Clause

Some argue that DOMA is an unconstitutional exercise of Congress's authority under the Full Faith and Credit Clause of the U.S. Constitution,[38] which states:

> Full Faith and Credit shall be given in each State to the public Acts, Records, and judicial Proceedings of every other State; And the Congress may by general Laws prescribe the Manner in which such Acts, Records and Proceedings shall be proved, and the Effect thereof.

Opponents argue that, although Congress has authority to pass laws that enable acts, judgments and the like to be given effect in other states, it has no constitutional power to pass a law permitting states to deny full faith and credit to another state's laws and judgments.[39] Conversely, some argue that DOMA does nothing more than simply restate the power granted to the states by the Full Faith and Credit Clause.[40] While there is no judicial precedent on this issue, Congress's general authority to "prescribe ... the effect" of public acts arguably gives it discretion to define the "effect" so that a particular public act is not due full faith and credit. Thus, plain reading of the clause appears to encompass both expansion and contraction.[41]

Equal Protection

Congress's authority to legislate in this manner under the Full Faith and Credit Clause, if the analysis set out above is accepted, does not conclude the matter. There are multiple constitutional constraints upon federal legislation. One that is relevant is the Equal Protection Clause in the Fourteenth Amendment and the effect of the Supreme Court's decision in *Romer v. Evans*,[42] which struck down a referendum-adopted provision of the Colorado Constitution, which repealed local ordinances that provided civil-rights protections for gay persons and which prohibited all governmental action designed to protect gays and lesbians from discrimination. The Court held that, under the Equal Protection Clause, legislation adverse to homosexuals was to be scrutinized under a "rational basis" standard of review.[43] The classification failed to pass even this deferential standard of review, because it imposed a special disability on homosexuals not visited on any other class of people and it could not be justified by any of the arguments made by the state. The state argued that its purpose for the amendment was two-fold: (1) to respect the freedom of association rights of other citizens, such as landlords and employers who objected to homosexuality; and (2) to serve the state's interest in conserving resources to fight discrimination against other protected groups.

DOMA can be distinguished from the Colorado amendment. DOMA's legislative history indicates that it was intended to protect federalism interests and state sovereignty in the area of domestic relations, historically a subject of almost exclusive state concern. Moreover, it permits but does not require states to deny recognition to same-sex marriages in other states, affording states with strong public policy concerns the discretion to effectuate that policy. Thus, it can be argued that DOMA is grounded not in hostility to homosexuals but in an intent to afford the states the discretion to act as their public policy on same-sex marriage dictates.

Substantive Due Process (Right to Privacy)

Another potential constitutional constraint is the Due Process Clause of the Fourteenth Amendment and the effect of the Supreme Court's decision in *Lawrence v. Texas*,[44] which struck down under the Due Process Clause a state statute criminalizing certain private sexual acts between homosexuals. The Court held that the Fourteenth Amendment's Due Process privacy guarantee extends to protect consensual sex between adult homosexuals. The Court noted that the Due Process right to privacy protects certain personal decisions from governmental interference. These personal decisions include issues regarding contraceptives, abortion, marriage, procreation, and family relations.[45] The Court extended this right to privacy to cover adult consensual homosexual sodomy.

It is currently unclear what impact, if any, the Court's decision in *Lawrence* will have on legal challenges to laws prohibiting same-sex marriage. On the one hand, this decision can be viewed as affirming a broad constitutional right to sexual privacy. Conversely, the Court distinguished this case from cases involving minors and "whether the government must give formal recognition to any relationship that homosexual persons seek to enter."[46] Courts may seek to distinguish statutes prohibiting same-sex marriage from statutes criminalizing homosexual conduct. Courts may view the preservation of the institution of marriage as sufficient justification for statutes banning same-sex marriage. Moreover, courts may view the public recognition of marriage differently than the sexual conduct of homosexuals in the privacy of their own homes.[47]

Interstate Recognition of Marriage

DOMA opponents take the position that the Full Faith and Credit Clause would obligate states to recognize same-sex marriages contracted in other states in which they are authorized. This conclusion is far from evident as this clause applies principally to the interstate recognition and enforcement of judgments.[48] It is settled law that final judgments are entitled to full faith and credit, regardless of other states' public policies, provided the issuing state had jurisdiction over the parties and the subject matter.[49] The Full Faith and Credit Clause has rarely been used by courts to validate marriages because marriages are not "legal judgments."

Questions concerning the validity of an out-of-state marriage are generally resolved without reference to the Full Faith and Credit Clause. In the legal sense, marriage is a "civil contract" created by the state which establishes certain duties and confers certain benefits.[50] Validly entering the contract creates the marital status; the duties and benefits attached by a state are incidents of that status. As such, the general tendency, based on comity rather than on compulsion under the Full Faith and Credit Clause, is to recognize marriages contracted in other states even if they could not have been celebrated in the recognizing state.

The general rule of validation for marriage is to look to the law of the place where the marriage was celebrated. A marriage satisfying the contracting state's requirements will usually be held valid everywhere.[51] Many states provide by statute that a marriage that is valid where contracted is valid within the state. This "place of celebration" rule is then subject to a number of exceptions, most of which are narrowly construed. The most common exception to the "place of celebration" rule is for marriages deemed contrary to the forum's strong public policy. Several states, such as Connecticut,[52] Idaho,[53] Illinois,[54] Kansas,[55] Missouri,[56] Pennsylvania,[57] South Carolina,[58] and Tennessee[59] provide an exception to this general rule by declaring out-of-state marriages void if against the state's public policy or if entered into with the intent to evade the law of the state. This exception applies only where another state's law violates "some fundamental principle of justice, some prevalent conception of good morals, some deep-rooted tradition of the common weal."[60]

Section 283 of the Restatement (Second) of Law provides:

> (1) The validity of marriage will be determined by the local law of the state which, with respect to the particular issue, has the most significant relationship to the spouses and the marriage under the principles stated in § 6.
>
> (2) A marriage which satisfies the requirements of the state where the marriage was contracted will everywhere be recognized as valid unless it violates the strong public policy of another state which had the most significant relationship to the spouses and the marriage at the time of the marriage.

STATES' RESPONSES

State Litigation

Massachusetts, unlike 26 states and the federal government, has not adopted a "defense of marriage statute" defining marriage as a union between a man and woman.[61] On April 11, 2001, a Boston-based, homosexual rights group, Gay and Lesbian Advocates and Defenders (GLAD) filed suit against the Massachusetts Department of Public Health on behalf of seven same-sex couples. The plaintiffs claimed that "refusing same-sex couples the opportunity to apply for a marriage license" violates Massachusetts' law and various portions of the Massachusetts Constitution. GLAD 's brief argued the existence of a fundamental right to marry "the person of one's choosing" in the due process provisions of the Massachusetts Constitution and asserted that the marriage laws, which allow both men and women to marry, violate equal protection provisions.[62]

The Superior Court rejected the plaintiffs' arguments after exploring the application of the word marriage, the construction of marriage statutes and finally, the historical purpose of marriage. The trial court found that based on history and the actions of the people's elected representatives, a right to same-sex marriage was not so rooted in tradition that a failure to recognize it violated fundamental liberty, nor was it implicit in ordered liberty.[63] Moreover, the court held that in excluding same-sex couples from marriage, the Commonwealth did not deprive them of substantive due process, liberty, or freedom of speech or association.[64] The court went on to find that limiting marriage to opposite-sex couples was rationally related to a legitimate state interest in encouraging procreation.[65]

On November 18, 2003, the Massachusetts Supreme Judicial Court overruled the lower court and held that, under the Massachusetts Constitution, the Commonwealth could not deny the protections, benefits, and obligations attendant on marriage to two individuals of the same sex who wish to marry.[66] The court concluded that interpreting the statutory term "marriage" to apply only to male-female unions lacked a rational basis for either due process or equal protection purposes under the state's constitution. Moreover, the court found that such a limitation was not justified by the state's interest in providing a favorable setting for procreation and had no rational relationship to the state's interests in ensuring that children be raised in optimal settings and in conservation of state and private financial resources.[67] The court reasoned that the laws of civil marriage did not privilege procreative heterosexual intercourse, nor contain any requirement that applicants for marriage licenses attest to their ability or intention to conceive children by coitus. Moreover, the court reasoned that the state has no power to provide varying levels of protection to children based on the circumstances of birth. As for the state's interest in conserving scarce state and private financial resources, the court found that the state failed to produce any evidence to support its assertion that same-sex couples were less financially interdependent than opposite-sex couples. In addition, Massachusetts marriage laws do not condition receipt of public and private financial benefits to married individuals on a demonstration of financial dependence on each other.[68] As this decision is based on the Commonwealth's constitution, it is not reviewable by the U.S. Supreme Court. The court stayed its decision for 180 days to give the Legislature time to enact legislation "as it may deem appropriate in light of this opinion."[69]

On February 3, 2004, the court ruled, in an advisory opinion to the state senate, that civil unions are not the constitutional equivalent of civil marriage.[70] The court reasoned that the establishment of civil unions for same-sex couples would create a separate class of citizens by status discrimination which would violate the equal protection and due process requirements of the Constitution of the Commonwealth.[71]

In the years following the Massachusetts decision, state Supreme Courts in New Jersey, California, Connecticut, and Iowa addressed the issue of same-sex marriage.[72] The California and Connecticut cases posed a slightly different question than the one presented in Massachusetts and Iowa, as California and Connecticut legislatures enacted parallel statutory schemes in the form of domestic partnerships and civil unions granting the states' same-sex couples the same rights and benefits as well as the obligations of civil marriage. As such, the legal issue before the California and Connecticut Supreme Courts was whether, in light of both marriage and domestic partnership/civil union statutes, the failure to designate the official relationship of same-sex couples as marriage violates the states' constitutions.[73]

While the California Supreme Court held that the privacy, due process, and equal protection provisions of the state's constitution guarantee the basic right of civil marriage to all individuals and couples regardless of their sexual orientation,[74] the Connecticut and Iowa Supreme Courts focused on the equal protection provision of their state constitutions.[75] In addressing the privacy and due process challenges, the California majority first looked at the nature and scope of the "right to marry." Relying on judicial precedent and legislative history,[76] the court concluded that the fundamental nature of the substantive rights embodied in the right to marry, and their central importance to one's opportunity to live a happy, meaningful, and satisfying life as a full member of society, require that the state constitution be interpreted to protect this right not to be "eliminated or abrogated by the Legislature or by the electorate through the statutory initiative process."[77] In reaching its conclusion, the court discussed the societal benefits of marriage, including child welfare and the role that marriage plays in "facilitating a stable family setting."[78] Furthermore, the court described marriage as the "basic unit" or "building block" of society.[79] The court noted that while marriage serves a vital societal interest, judicial precedent also demonstrated that the right to marry is an "integral component of an individual's interest in personal autonomy" protected by the privacy and liberty interest provisions of the California constitution. [80]

While the California court acknowledged that the constitutional right to marry did not obligate the state to afford specific tax or other governmental benefits on the basis of a couple's family relation, the right to marry does "obligate the state to take affirmative action to grant official, public recognition to the couple's relationship as a family."[81] Thus, the court concluded that the California constitution guarantees same-sex couples the same "substantive constitutional rights as opposite-sex couples to choose one's life partner and enter with that person in a committed, officially recognized, and protected family relationship that enjoys all of the constitutionally based incidents of marriage."[82]

In addressing the equal protection question, the California Supreme Court used a different standard of review than the Connecticut and Iowa Supreme Courts. In a matter of first impression, the California Supreme Court determined that strict scrutiny was the appropriate standard of review for sexual orientation discrimination. According to the California court, classification or discrimination on the basis of sexual orientation is analogous to race, gender,[83] or religious discrimination, as these types of classifications are based on characteristics that bear no relationship to one's ability to perform or contribute to society.[84] As such, the California court expanded protection against sexual orientation discrimination by determining that strict scrutiny was the appropriate review.

Under the heightened standard of strict scrutiny, the state had to establish (1) a compelling state interest, and (2) that the differential treatment was necessary to achieve the compelling state interest. The court concluded that the designation of "marriage" would not have an impact on opposite-sex couples. However, the court concluded that a separate and differently named family for same-sex couples would be harmful to the couples as well as their offspring due to a possible perception that such a union is of a "lesser stature" in comparison to relationships of opposite-sex couples. The court concluded that the state's domestic partnership law provides insufficient protections to same-sex couples. Specifically, the court stated that "[r]etaining the designation of marriage exclusively for opposite-sex couples and providing only a separate and distinct designation for same-sex couples may well have the effect of perpetuating a more general premise—now emphatically rejected by this state—that gay individuals and same-sex couples are in some respects 'second-class citizens.'" As such, the court found such a distinction unconstitutional under the California constitution.

On November 4, 2008, California voters approved a constitutional amendment (Proposition 8) limiting the validity and recognition of "marriages" to heterosexual couples. This constitutional amendment appears to be intended to overrule the California Supreme Court's decision. However, legal challenges were filed seeking injunctive relief against the amendment's implementation. On November 19, 2008, the court denied the requests for injunctive relief. However, the court agreed to decide three issues regarding Proposition 8's validity and/or retroactivity, including (1) whether Proposition 8 was a constitutional amendment or revision, (2) the validity of the initiative process itself, and (3) whether Proposition 8 itself is retroactive, applying to existing same-sex marriages.[85]

On May 26, 2009, the California Supreme Court concluded that Proposition 8 is a properly enacted limited constitutional amendment, not a constitutional revision requiring a two-thirds vote of the legislature to be placed before voters.[86] The court noted that precedent establishes the criteria for determining whether a constitutional change constitutes a revision rather than an amendment. A court must assess "(1) the meaning and scope of the constitutional change at issue, and (2) the effect – both quantitative and qualitative – that the constitutional change will have on the basic governmental plan or framework embodied in the preexisting provisions of the California Constitution."[87] Concluding that Proposition 8 is a constitutional amendment, the court analyzed its quantitative and qualitative effect on the preexisting provisions of the state constitution and reasoned that the amendment does not repeal or abrogate same-sex couples' constitutional rights of privacy and due process or fundamentally alter "the meaning and substance" of equal protection principles recognized in the court's previous ruling pertaining to same-sex marriage and in laws allowing civil unions. Instead, the court stated that

> [t]he measure carves out a narrow and limited exception to the state constitutional rights, reserving the official designation of the term 'marriage' for the union of opposite-sex couples as a matter of state constitutional law, but leaving undisturbed all of the other extremely significant aspects of a same-sex couple's state constitutional right to establish an officially recognized and protected family relationship and the guarantee of equal protection of the laws.[88]

Unlike its previous decision, the court did not explicitly address whether a parallel structure, such as a civil union, would maintain same-sex couples' constitutional privacy, due process, and equal protection rights. However, it might be inferred from the court's characterization of Proposition 8[89] that it now believes that a parallel structure would comport with constitutional requirements.

In addressing the status of same-sex marriages performed before Proposition 8's passage, the court unanimously found that the amendment applies prospectively. The court noted that ending such marriages would be akin to "throwing property rights into disarray, destroying the legal interests and expectations of thousands of couples and their families, and potentially undermining the ability of citizens to plan their lives according to the law as it has been determined by the state's highest court."[90] As such, the court held that such marriages remain valid and must continue to be recognized within the state.[91]

The Connecticut and Iowa Supreme Courts agreed with the California Supreme Court's finding that laws discriminating against homosexuals must be subjected to a higher level of scrutiny. However, these courts declined to use a strict scrutiny analysis. Instead, the courts used a variety of factors to determine that sexual orientation is a quasi-suspect class analogous to gender, thus warranting an intermediate scrutiny analysis.[92] In exploring the nature of homosexual identity, the history of societal views regarding homosexuality, and the limitation of political power possessed by homosexuals, the courts found that homosexuals suffered a history of invidious discrimination based on characteristics not within their control that bear "no relation to [their] ability to perform or contribute to society."[93] Therefore, the courts concluded that homosexuals are a quasi-suspect class requiring the state to advance a sufficiently persuasive justification for denying same-sex couples the right to marry. As in the Massachusetts and California decisions, the Connecticut and Iowa Supreme Courts rejected the state's justifications of promoting uniformity and preserving the traditional definition of marriage.[94]

Similarly, on October 25, 2006, the New Jersey Supreme Court held that the state's constitution requires that same-sex couples be granted the same legal rights as married heterosexual couples. However, the court declined to label those rights and instead ordered the state legislature to amend its marriage statutes or enact a new statutory scheme granting the state's same-sex couples the rights of married couples within 180 days.[95]

In its 4-3 decision,[96] the majority separated the plaintiffs' equal protection argument into two questions: (1) whether committed same-sex couples have a constitutional right to the benefits and privileges afforded to married heterosexual couples and (2) if so, whether they have the constitutional right to have their permanent committed relationship recognized by the name "marriage."[97] In addressing the first question, the court discussed New Jersey's recent history of passing laws providing benefits to same-sex couples. For example, the state forbids sexual orientation discrimination and allows same-sex couples to become foster parents as well as adopt children. The court concluded that the state's statutes and judicial opinions provide committed same-sex couples with a strong interest in equality of treatment.[98] Moreover, the court concluded that although the state's Domestic Partnership Act provided same-sex couples with some important rights, the act failed to "bridge the inequality gap between committed same-sex couples and married opposite-sex couples."[99]

The court held that the state has no legitimate interest in denying the benefits and privileges of marriage to same-sex couples.[100] In assessing the public need for denying committed same-sex couples the full benefits and privileges that flow from marriage, the court rejected the state's argument of uniformity with other states and concluded that the disparate treatment of committed same-sex couples directly disadvantages their children. Moreover, the court concluded that there "is no rational basis for, on the one hand, giving gays and lesbians full civil rights in their status as individuals, and, on the other, giving them an incomplete set of rights when they follow the inclination of their sexual orientation and enter into committed same-sex relationships."[101] As such, the court found that denying committed same-sex couples the financial and social benefits and privileges given to married heterosexual couples bears no substantial relationship to a legitimate government purpose.

However, the court held that there is no fundamental due process right to same-sex marriage encompassed within the concept of "liberty" guaranteed by the state constitution. In reaching its decision, the court adopted the general standard followed by the U.S. Supreme Court in construing the Due Process Clause of the Fourteenth Amendment of the U.S. Constitution. The court found that there was no legal or historical basis for same-sex marriage nor anything to suggest that the framers of the federal or state constitutions considered it a fundamental right to be afforded special protection. The court emphasized the importance of tradition to substantive due process analysis—and held that, according to tradition, the right to marry a same-sex partner is not "deeply rooted in our nation's history."[102] As a result, the court declined to find a fundamental right to same-sex marriage. Instead, the court ordered the legislature to provide to committed same-sex couples the "full rights and benefits enjoyed by heterosexual couples."[103] The court provided two options to the legislature: (1) amend the marriage statutes to include same-sex couples; or (2) enact a parallel statutory structure by another name, in which same-sex couples would receive the same rights and benefits as well as the "burdens and obligations of civil marriage."[104]

Although the aforementioned opinions deal exclusively with a state constitution,[105] an Arizona Court of Appeals, exercising its discretion to accept jurisdiction based on the issue of first impression, held that the fundamental right to marry protected by the Fourteenth Amendment of the U.S. Constitution as well as the Arizona Constitution did not encompass the right to marry a same-sex partner.[106] Moreover, the court found that the state had a legitimate interest in encouraging procreation and child rearing within the marital relationship and limiting that relationship to opposite-sex couples.

In light of the Supreme Court's decision in *Lawrence*, the petitioners argued that the Arizona statute prohibiting same-sex marriages violated their fundamental right to marry and their right to equal protection under the laws, both of which are guaranteed by the federal and state constitutions. The

Arizona court rejected the petitioners' argument that the Supreme Court in *Lawrence* implicitly recognized that the fundamental right to marry includes the freedom to choose a same-sex spouse.[107] The court viewed the *Lawrence* language as acknowledging a homosexual person's "right to define his or her own existence, and achieve the type of individual fulfillment that is the hallmark of a free society, by entering a homosexual relationship."[108] However, the court declined to view the language as stating that such a right includes the choice to enter a state-sanctioned, same-sex marriage.[109]

As such, the court reviewed the constitutionality of the challenged statutes using a rational basis analysis and found that the state has a legitimate interest in encouraging procreation and child- rearing within the marital relationship, and that limiting marriage to opposite-sex couples is rationally related to that interest. Moreover, the court said that while the state's reasoning is debatable, it is not arbitrary or irrational. Consequently, the court upheld the challenged statutes.

While the aforementioned states addressed the legalization of same-sex marriages judicially, Vermont addressed the issue legislatively. On April 7, 2009, state legislators garnered a sufficient number of votes to override the governor's veto. On May 6, 2009, Maine's governor signed a bill legalizing same-sex marriages in the state.

State Constitutional Amendments Limiting Marriage to a Man and a Woman

Alabama

Marriage is inherently a unique relationship between a man and a woman. As a matter of public policy, this state has a special interest in encouraging, supporting, and protecting this unique relationship in order to promote, among other goals, the stability and welfare of society and its children. A marriage contracted between individuals of the same sex is invalid in this state.

Marriage is a sacred covenant, solemnized between a man and a woman, which, when the legal capacity and consent of both parties is present, establishes their relationship as husband and wife, and which is recognized by the state as a civil contract.

No marriage license shall be issued in the State of Alabama to parties of the same sex.

The State of Alabama shall not recognize as valid any marriage of parties of the same sex that occurred or was alleged to have occurred as a result of the law of any jurisdiction regardless of whether a marriage license was issued.

The State of Alabama shall not recognize as valid any common law marriage of parties of the same sex.

A union replicating marriage of or between persons of the same sex in the State of Alabama or in any other jurisdiction shall be considered and treated in all respects as having no legal force or effect in this state and shall not be recognized by this state as a marriage or other union replicating marriage.[110]

Arkansas

Marriage consists only of the union of one man and one woman. Legal status for unmarried persons which is identical or substantially similar to marital status shall not be valid or recognized in Arkansas, except that the Legislature may recognize a common law marriage from another state between a man and a woman. The Legislature has the power to determine the capacity of persons to marry, subject to this amendment, and the legal rights, obligations, privileges and immunities of marriage.[111]

Arizona

Only a union of one man and one woman shall be valid or recognized as marriage in this state.[112]

California

Only marriage between a man and a woman is valid and recognized in California.[113]

Colorado

Only a union of one man and one woman shall be valid or recognized as a marriage in this state.[114]

Florida

Inasmuch as marriage is the legal union of only one man and one woman as husband and wife, no other legal union that is treated as marriage or the substantial equivalent thereof shall be valid or recognized.[115]

Georgia

This state shall recognize as marriage only the union of man and woman. Marriages between persons of the same sex are prohibited in this state. No union between persons of the same sex shall be recognized by this state as entitled to the benefits of marriage. This state shall not give effect to any public act, record or judicial proceeding of any other state or jurisdiction respecting a relationship between persons of the same sex that is treated as a marriage under the laws of such other state or jurisdiction. The courts of this state shall have no jurisdiction to grant a divorce or separate maintenance with respect to any such relationship or otherwise to consider or rule on any of the parties' respective rights arising as a result of or in connection with such relationship.[116]

Idaho

A marriage between a man and a woman is the only domestic legal union that shall be valid or recognized in this state.[117]

Kansas

The marriage contract is to be considered in law as a civil contract. Marriage shall be constituted by one man and one woman only. All other marriages are declared to be contrary to the public policy of this state and are void.

No relationship, other than a marriage, shall be recognized by the state as entitling the parties to the rights or incidents of marriage.[118]

Kentucky

Only a marriage between one man and one woman shall be valid or recognized as a marriage in Kentucky. A legal status identical or substantially similar to that of marriage for unmarried individuals shall not be valid or recognized.[119]

Louisiana

Marriage in the state of Louisiana shall consist only of the union of one man and one woman. No official or court of the state of Louisiana shall construe this constitution or any state law to require that marriage or the legal incidents thereof be conferred upon any member of a union other than the union of one man and one woman. A legal status identical or substantially similar to that of marriage for unmarried individuals shall not be valid or recognized. No official or court of the state of Louisiana shall recognize any marriage contracted in any other jurisdiction which is not the union of one man and one woman to the state constitution.[120]

Michigan

To secure and preserve the benefits of marriage for our society and for future generations of children, the union of one man and one woman in marriage shall be the only agreement recognized as a marriage or similar union for any purpose.[121]

Mississippi

Marriage may take place and may be valid under the laws of this state only between a man and a woman. A marriage in another state or foreign jurisdiction between persons of the same gender, regardless of when the marriage took place, may not be recognized in this state and is void and unenforceable under the laws of this state.[122]

Missouri

That to be valid and recognized in this state, a marriage shall exist only between a man and a woman.[123]

Montana

Only a marriage between one man and one woman shall be valid or recognized as a marriage in this state.

North Dakota

Marriage consists only of the legal union between a man and a woman. No other domestic union, however denominated, may be recognized as a marriage or given the same or substantially equivalent effect.

Ohio

Only a union between one man and one woman may be a marriage valid in or recognized by this state and its political subdivisions. This state and its political subdivisions shall not create or recognize a legal status for relationships of unmarried individuals that intends to approximate the design, qualities, significance or effect of marriage.

Oklahoma

Marriage in this state shall consist only of the union of one man and one woman. Neither this constitution nor any other provision of law shall be construed to require that marital status or the legal incidents thereof be conferred upon unmarried couples or groups. A marriage between persons of the same gender performed in another state shall not be recognized as valid and binding in this state as of the date of the marriage. Any person knowingly issuing a marriage license in violation of this section shall be guilty of a misdemeanor.[124]

Oregon

It is the policy of Oregon, and its political subdivisions, that only a marriage between one man and one woman shall be valid or legally recognized as a marriage.[125]

South Carolina

Marriage in the state of South Carolina, and its political subdivisions, is exclusively defined as a union between one man and one woman; all other attempted or putative unions, including those recognized by other jurisdictions are void ab initio.[126]

South Dakota

Only marriage between a man and a woman shall be valid or recognized in South Dakota. The uniting of two or more persons in a civil union, domestic partnership, or other quasi- marital relationship shall not be valid or recognized in South Dakota.[127]

Tennessee

The historical institution and legal contract solemnizing the relationship of one man and one woman shall be the only legally recognized marital contract in this state. Any policy or law or judicial interpretation, purporting to define marriage as anything other than the historical institution and legal contract between one man and one woman, is contrary to the public policy of this state and shall be void and unenforceable in Tennessee. If another state or foreign jurisdiction issues a license for persons to marry and if such marriage is prohibited in this state by the provisions of this section, then the marriage shall be void and unenforceable in this state.[128]

Texas

Marriage in this state shall consist only of the union of one man and one woman. This state or a political subdivision of this state may not create or recognize any legal status identical or similar to marriage.[129]

Utah

Marriage consists only of the legal union between a man and a woman. No other domestic status or union, however denominated, between persons is valid or recognized or may be authorized, sanctioned or given the same or substantially equivalent legal effect as a marriage.[130]

Virginia

Only a union between one man and one woman may be a marriage valid in or recognized by this Commonwealth and its political subdivisions. This Commonwealth and its political subdivisions shall not create or recognize a legal status for relationships of unmarried individuals that intends to approximate the design, qualities, significance, or effects of marriage. Nor shall this Commonwealth or its political subdivisions create or recognize another union, partnership, or other legal status to which is assigned the rights, benefits, obligations, qualities, or effects of marriage.[131]

Wisconsin

Only a marriage between one man and one woman shall be valid or recognized as a marriage in this state. A legal status identical or substantially similar to that of marriage for unmarried individuals shall not be valid or recognized in this state.[132]

State "Civil Union" Laws

Civil union/domestic partnership laws confer certain rights and benefits upon domestic partners which vary depending on state law. Some of these rights and benefits include laws relating to title, tenure, descent and distribution, intestate succession; causes of action related to or dependent upon spousal status,[133] including an action for wrongful death,[134] emotional distress, or loss of consortium; probate law and procedure; adoption law and procedure; insurance benefits; workers' compensation rights; laws relating to medical care and treatment, hospital visitation and notification; family leave benefits; public assistance benefits under state laws and laws relating to state taxes.[135]

For example, in Vermont, civil union status[136] is available to two persons of the same sex who are unrelated[137] and affords parties "the same benefits, protections and responsibilities under Vermont law, whether they derive from statute, policy, administrative or court rule, common law or any other source of civil law, as are granted to spouses in a marriage."[138] Civil union status is also available in Connecticut,[139] New Hampshire,[140] and New Jersey.[141] Domestic partnership laws in California,[142] Hawaii,[143] New Jersey,[144] Oregon,[145] and Washington[146] also offer some marital benefits to same-sex couples, although not as comprehensive as Vermont's or Connecticut's civil unions.[147]

CONGRESSIONAL ACTIVITY

No bills have been introduced in the 111th Congress which address the issue of same-sex marriage. However, several bills were introduced in previous Congresses.[148] For example, in the 110th Congress, H.J.Res. 22, a proposed amendment to the U.S. Constitution was introduced. The text of the proposed amendment is as follows:

> Section 1. Marriage in the United States shall consist only of a legal union of one man and one woman.
>
> Section 2. No court of the United States or of any State shall have jurisdiction to determine whether this Constitution or the constitution of any State requires that the legal incidents of marriage be conferred upon any union other than a legal union between one man and one woman.
>
> Section 3. No State shall be required to give effect to any public act, record, or judicial proceeding of any other State concerning a union between persons of the same sex that is treated as a marriage, or as having the legal incidents of marriage, under the laws of such other State.

Also introduced in the 110th, H.R. 107 would have defined marriage for all legal purposes in the District of Columbia to consist of the union of one man and one woman.[149] H.R. 724, introduced in January 2007, would have amended Title 28 of the United State Code to limit federal court jurisdiction over questions under DOMA.[150]

Although national uniformity may be achieved upon ratification of one of the proposed amendments to the U.S. Constitution,[151] states would no longer have the flexibility of defining marriage within their borders. Moreover, states may be prohibited from recognizing a same-sex marriage performed and recognized outside of the United States.[152] Some of the proposed amendments may affect a state's ability to define civil unions or domestic partnerships and the benefits conferred upon such.

A further complication in the definition of marriage may arise regarding the determination of an individual's gender. As the first official document to indicate a person's sex, the designation on the birth certificate "usually controls the sex designation on all later documents."[153] Some courts have held that sexual identity for purposes of marriage is determined by the sex stated on the birth certificate, regardless of subsequent sexual reassignment.[154] However, some argue that this method is flawed, as an infant's sex may be misidentified at birth and the individual may subsequently identify with and conform his or her biology to another sex upon adulthood.[155]

Table 1. State Statutes Defining "Marriage"

State	Statute	Marriage Definition[a]	Non-Recognition
Alabama	ALA. CODE § 30-1-19 (2003)	X	X
Alaska	ALASKA STAT. § 25.05.011 (2003)	X	
Arizona	ARIZ. REV. STAT. § 25-101 (2003)		X
Arkansas	ARK. CODE ANN. § 9-11 -109 (2003)	X	
California	Judicial Interpretation	X[b]	
Colorado	COLO. REV. STAT. § 14-2-104 (2003)	X	
Connecticut	Judicial Interpretation		X[c]
Delaware	DEL. CODE ANN. tit. 13 § 101 (2002)		X
Florida	FLA. STAT. Ch. 741.04 (2002)	X	
Georgia	GA. CODE ANN. § 19-3-3.1 (2002)		X

Table 1. (Continued)

State	Statute	Marriage Definition[a]	Non-Recognition
Hawaii	Haw. Rev. Stat. Ann. § 572-1 (2003)	X	
Idaho*	IDAHO CODE § 32-209 (2003)	X	
Illinois*	750 ILL. COMP. STAT. 5/201 (2003)	X	X
Indiana	IND. CODE ANN. § 31-1 1-1-1 (2003)	X	X
Iowa	IOWA CODE § 595.2 (2003)	X[d]	
Kansas*	KAN. STAT. ANN. § 23-101 (2002)	X	
Kentucky	KY. REV. STAT. ANN. § 402.020 (2002)		X
Louisiana	LA. CIV. CODE art. 86 (2003)	X	
Maine	ME. REV. STAT. ANN. tit. 19, § 701 (2003)	X[e]	
Maryland	Md. Code Ann. Fam. Law § 2-201 (2002)	X	
Massachusetts	Judicial Interpretation	X[f]	
Michigan	Mich. Comp. Laws § 551.1 (2003)	X	X
Minnesota	MINN. STAT. § 517.01 (2002)	X	
Mississippi	MISS. CODE ANN. § 93-1 - 1 (2003)		X
Missouri*	MO. REV. STAT. § 451.022 (2003)		X
Montana	MONT. CODE ANN. § 40-1 - 103 (2002)	X	
Nebraska	NEB. REV. STAT. ANN. ART. 1, § 29 (2002)		X
Nevada	Nev. Rev. Stat. Ann. § 122.020 (2003)	X	
New Hampshire	N.H. Rev. Stat. Ann. § 457:2 (2002)	X[g]	X
New Jersey	Judicial Interpretation	X[h]	
New Mexico	N.M. STAT. ANN § 40-1 - 1 (2002)	X[i]	

Table 1. (Continued)

State	Statute	Marriage Definition[a]	Non-Recognition
New York	Judicial Interpretation	X[j]	
North Carolina	N.C. GEN. STAT. § 51-1.2 (2003)		X
North Dakota	N.D. CENT. CODE § 14-03-01 (2002)	X	
Ohio*	Ohio Rev. Code Ann. §3101	X[k]	X
Oklahoma	OKLA. STAT. tit. 43 § 3.1 (2003)		X
Oregon	OR. REV. STAT. § 106.010 (2001)	X[l]	
Pennsylvania*	PA. STAT. ANN. tit. 23 § 1704 (2002)		X
Rhode Island	R.I. GEN. LAWS § 15-1 - 1 (2002)	X[m]	
South Carolina*	S.C. CODE ANN. § 20-1 -10 (2002)		X
South Dakota	S. D. CODIFIED LAWS § 25-1 - 1 (2002)	X	
Tennessee*	TENN. CODE. ANN. § 36-3-113 (2003)	X	
Texas	Tex. Fam. Code Ann. § 2.001 (2002)	X	
Utah	UTAH CODE ANN. § 30-1-2 (2003)		X
Vermont	VT. STAT. ANN. tit. 15 § 8 (2003)	X[n]	
Virginia	VA. CODE ANN. § 20-45.2 (2003)		X
Washington	WASH. REV. CODE ANN. § 26.04.010 (2003)	X	
West Virginia	W. VA. CODE § 48-2-603 (2003)		X
Wisconsin	Wis. Stat. § 765.01 (2002)	X[o]	
Wyoming	WYO. STAT. § 20-1-101 (2003)	X	
Puerto Rico	P.R. LAWS ANN. tit. 31, § 221 (2002)	X	

Notes: States in bold have constitutional amendments prohibiting same-sex marriage. States marked with an asterisk have a statute establishing same-sex unions as a violation of the state's public policy.

a. Marriage consists of a contract between one man and one woman.

b. In *In re Marriage Cases*, 183 P.3d 384 (Ca. 2008), the court held that the state's constitution guarantees the basic right to civil marriage to all individuals and couples regardless of their sexual orientation. In November 2008, voters approved a constitutional amendment which recognizes as valid marriages unions of heterosexual couples. On May 26, 2009, the court found the ban is a permissible and valid amendment under the state's constitution. Strauss v. Horton, 2009 WL 1444594 (Ca. May 26, 2009).

c. In *Kerrigan v. Commissioner of Public Health*, 2008 WL 4530885 (Oct. 28, 2008), the court held that laws restricting civil marriage to heterosexual couples violate the state's equal protection provision.

d. In *Varnum v. Brien*, 2009 WL 87044 (April 3, 2009), the court held that laws restricting civil marriage to heterosexual couples violate the state's equal protection clause.

e. On May 6, 2009, Maine's governor signed a bill legalizing same-sex marriages.

f. The Supreme Judicial Court has interpreted "marriage," within Massachusetts' statutes, "as the union of one man and one woman." *Adoption of Tammy*, 619 N.E.2d 315 (1993). However, in *Goodridge v. Dept. of Public Health*, 798 N.E.2d 941 (Mass. 2003), the court construed the term "marriage" to mean the voluntary union of two persons as spouses, to the exclusion of all others.

g. On June 4, 2009, New Hampshire's governor signed a bill legalizing same-sex marriages.

h. The New Jersey Supreme Court held that the state's constitution requires that same-sex couples be granted the same rights as married heterosexual couples. The Court left the definition of marriage to the legislature. *Lewis v. Harris*, 908 A.2d 1196 (N.J. 2006). On December 15, 2006, the legislature declined to expand the term "marriage" to include same sex couples. Instead, the legislature created a civil union status for same-sex couples effective February 2007.

i. Marriage is a civil contract requiring consent of parties.

j. Marriage has been traditionally defined as the voluntary union of one man and one woman as husband and wife. See, for example, Fisher v. Fisher, 250 N.Y. 313, 165 N. E. 460 (1929). A basic assumption, therefore, is that one of the two parties to the union must be male and the other must be female. On the basis of this assumption, the New York courts have consistently viewed it essential to the formation of a marriage that the parties be of opposite sexes.

k. Effective May 7, 2004.

i. Marriage is a civil contract entered into in person by males at least 1 7 years of age and females at least 17 years of age, who are otherwise capable, and solemnized in accordance with ORS 106.1.

m. Men are forbidden to marry kindred.

n. On April 7, 2009, Vermont became the first state to legalize same-sex marriages legislatively. State legislatures garnered a sufficient number of votes to override the governor's veto.

o. Marriage, so far as its validity at law is concerned, is a civil contract, to which the consent of the parties capable in law of contracting is essential, and which creates the legal status of husband and wife.

Conclusion

States currently possess the authority to decide whether to recognize an out-of-state marriage. The Full Faith and Credit Clause has rarely been used by states to validate marriages because marriages are not "legal judgments." With respect to cases decided under the Full Faith and Credit Clause that involve conflicting state statutes, the Supreme Court generally examines the significant aggregation of contacts the forum has with the parties and the occurrence or transaction to decide which state's law to apply. Similarly, based upon generally accepted legal principles, states routinely decide whether a marriage validly contracted in another jurisdiction will be recognized in-state by examining whether it has a significant relationship with the spouses and the marriage.

Congress is empowered under the Full Faith and Credit Clause of the Constitution to prescribe the manner that public acts, commonly understood to mean legislative acts, records, and proceedings shall be proved and the effect of such acts, records, and proceedings in other states.[156]

The Supreme Court's decisions in *Romer v. Colorado* and *Lawrence v. Texas* may present different issues concerning DOMA's constitutionality. Basically *Romer* appears to stand for the proposition that legislation targeting gays and lesbians is constitutionally impermissible under the Equal Protection Clause unless the legislative classification bears a rational relationship to a legitimate state purpose. Because same-sex marriages are singled out for differential treatment, DOMA appears to create a legislative classification for equal protection purposes that must meet a rational basis test. It is possible that DOMA would survive constitutional scrutiny under *Romer* inasmuch as the statute was enacted to protect the traditional institution of marriage. Moreover, DOMA does not prohibit states from recognizing same-sex marriage if they so choose.

Lawrence appears to stand for the proposition that the zone of privacy protected by the Due Process Clause of the Fourteen Amendment extends to adult, consensual sex between homosexuals. *Lawrence's* implication for statutes banning same-sex marriages and the constitutional validity of the DOMA are unclear.

End Notes

[1] *Goodridge v. Dept. of Public Health*, 798 N.E.2d 941 (Mass. 2003).

[2] *Lewis v. Harris*, 908 A.2d 196 (NJ 2006).
[3] *In re Marriage Cases*, 183 P.3d 384 (Ca. 2008).
[4] *Kerrigan v. Commissioner of Public Health*, 957 A.2d. 407 (Conn. 2008).
[5] *Varnum v. Brien*, No. 07-1499, 2009 WL 874044 (Iowa April 3, 2009).
[6] *Lewis v. Harris*, 908 A.2d 196 (NJ 2006).
[7] Voters approved the constitutional ban on June 6, 2006.
[8] Voters approved the constitutional ban on November 2, 2004.
[9] Voters approved the constitutional ban on November 4, 2008.
[10] Voters approved the constitutional ban on November 4, 2008. This vote appears to overrule the California State Supreme Court's decision in *In re Marriage Cases*, 183 P.3d 384 (Ca. 2008) granting same-sex couples the right to marry. On May 26, 2009, the California Supreme Court found the ban was a permissible and valid amendment under the state's constitution. However, the court unanimously held that the amendment applies prospectively and not retroactively. As such, the court upheld same-sex marriages entered into before the amendment's passage. *Strauss v. Horton*, 2009 WL 1444594 (Ca. May 26, 2009).
[11] Voters approved the constitutional ban on November 7, 2006.
[12] Voters approved the constitutional ban on November 4, 2008.
[13] Voters approved the constitutional ban on November 2, 2004.
[14] Voters approved the constitutional ban on November 7, 2006.
[15] Voters approved the constitutional ban on April 5, 2005.
[16] Voters approved the constitutional ban on November 2, 2004.
[17] Voters approved the constitutional ban on September 18, 2004. The Louisiana Supreme Court reversed a state district judge's ruling striking down the amendment on the grounds that it violated a provision of the state constitution requiring that an amendment cover only one subject. The Court found that each provision of the amendment is germane to the single object of defense of marriage and constitutes an element of the plan advanced to achieve this object. Forum for Equality *PAC v. McKeithen*, 893 So.3d 715 (La. 2005). Similarly, the Georgia Supreme Court reversed a lower court's ruling. *Perdue v. O'Kelley*, 280 GA 732 (GA. 2006). Other states that also have single-subject requirements, Ohio and Oklahoma, may face similar legal challenges.
[18] Voters approved the constitutional ban on November 2, 2004.
[19] Voters approved the constitutional ban on November 2, 2004.
[20] Voters approved the constitutional ban on August 3, 2004.
[21] Voters approved the constitutional ban on November 2, 2004.
[22] A U.S. district court judge struck down Nebraska's ban on gay marriage, saying that the ban "imposes significant burdens on both the expressive and intimate associational rights" of gays "and creates a significant barrier to the plaintiffs' right to petition or to participate in the political process." *Citizens for Equal Protection Inc., v. Bruning*, 368 F.Supp.2d 980 (D. NE May 12, 2005). However, the 8th Circuit Court of Appeals reversed finding that the Nebraska's constitutional amendment "and other laws limiting the state-recognized institution of marriage to heterosexual couples are rationally related to legitimate state interest and therefore do not violate the Constitution of the United States." *Citizens for Equal Protection Inc., v. Bruning*, 455 F.3d 859 (8th Cir. 2006).
[23] Voters approved the constitutional ban on November 2, 2004.
[24] Voters approved the constitutional ban on November 2, 2004.
[25] Voters approved the constitutional ban on November 2, 2004.
[26] Voters approved the constitutional ban on November 2, 2004. On April 4, 2005, the Oregon Supreme Court invalidated Multnomah County same-sex marriages, stating that the marriage licenses were issued to same-sex couples without authority and were void at the time they were issued. *Li v. State*, 110 P.3d 91 (Or. 2005).
[27] Voters approved the constitutional ban on November 7, 2006.
[28] Voters approved the constitutional ban on November 7, 2006.

[29] Voters approved the constitutional ban on November 7, 2006.

[30] Voters approved the constitutional ban on November 8, 2005.

[31] Voters approved the constitutional ban on November 7, 2006.

[32] Voters approved the constitutional ban on November 7, 2006.

[33] These states are Arizona, California, Delaware, Florida, Illinois, Indiana, Iowa, Maine, Maryland, Minnesota, New Hampshire, North Carolina, Pennsylvania, Vermont, Washington, West Virginia, and Wyoming.

[34] P.L. 104-199, 110 Stat. 2419 (codified at 1 U.S.C. § 7 and 28 U.S.C. § 1738C).

[35] 28 U.S.C. §1738C.

[36] 1 U.S.C. § 7.

[37] It should be noted that a federal bankruptcy court in the Western District of Washington found DOMA constitutional. Two American women, married in British Columbia, Canada filed a joint bankruptcy petition in Tacoma, challenging the definitional part of DOMA. The court ruled that there was no fundamental constitutional right to marry someone of the same sex and that DOMA did not violate the Fourth, Fifth or Tenth amendments, nor the principles of comity. *In re Lee Kandu and Ann C. Kandu*, No. 03-51312 (Western District of Washington, August 17, 2004). This decision is not binding on other courts.

In *Wilson v. Ake*, a same-sex couple sought a declaration that their marriage was valid for federal and Florida law purposes. To issue such a declaration, the court would have had to invalidate both the federal DOMA and the Florida statutes defining marriage the same way and expressly forbidding courts to recognize same-sex marriages from other states. The *Wilson* court declined to invalidate any of the relevant statutes finding that (1) DOMA did not violate the Full Faith and Credit Clause; (2) the right to marry a person of the same sex was not a fundamental right guaranteed by the Due Process Clause; (3) homosexuals were not a suspect class warranting strict scrutiny of equal protection claim; (4) under a rational basis analysis, DOMA did not violate equal protection or due process guarantees; and (5) the Florida statute prohibiting same-sex marriage is constitutional. *Wilson v. Ake*, 354 F.Supp.3d 1298 (M.D. Florida 2005). Moreover, the Wilson court found that it was bound by the U.S. Supreme Court's decision in *Baker v. Nelson*, 191 N.W.2d 185 (1971), *appeal dismissed*, 409 U.S. 810 (1972).

In *Baker v. Nelson*, two adult males' application for a marriage license was denied by the county clerk because the petitioners were of the same sex. The plaintiffs appealed to the Minnesota Supreme Court. Plaintiffs argued that Minnesota Statute § 517.08, which did not authorize marriage between persons of the same sex, violated the First, Eighth, Ninth and Fourteenth Amendments of the U.S. Constitution. The Minnesota Supreme Court rejected plaintiffs' assertion that "the right to marry without regard to the sex of the parties is a fundamental right of all persons" and held that § 517.08 did not violate the Due Process Clause or Equal Protection Clause. 191 N.W.2d at 186-87.

The plaintiffs appealed the Minnesota Supreme Court's ruling to the U.S. Supreme Court pursuant to 28 U.S.C. § 1257(2). Under 28 U.S.C. § 1257, the Supreme Court has discretion to refuse to adjudicate the case on its merits. The Supreme Court ultimately dismissed the appeal "for want of a substantial federal question." *Baker*, 409 U.S. at 810.

The *Wilson* court, relying on *Hicks v. Miranda* (422 U.S. 332 (1975)), found that a dismissal for lack of a substantial federal question constitutes an adjudication on the merits that is binding on lower federal courts.

[39] See 142 Cong. Rec. S593 1-33 (June 6, 1996) (statement introducing Professor Laurence H. Tribe's letter into the record concluding that DOMA "would be an unconstitutional attempt by Congress to limit the full faith and credit clause of the Constitution.").

[40] See Paige E. Chabora, Congress' Power Under the Full Faith and Credit Clause and the Defense of Marriage Act of 1996, 76 Neb. L. Rev. 604, 62 1-35 (1997).

[41] *See e.g., Wilson v. Ake*, 354 F.Supp.2d at 1302 (finding that DOMA was an appropriate exercise of Congress's power to regulate conflicts between the laws of different states, and holding otherwise would create "a license for a single State to create national policy.").

[42] 517 U.S. 620 (1996).

[43] *Id.*

[44] 539 U.S. 558 (2003). For a legal analysis of this decision, refer to CRS Report RL3 1681, *Homosexuality and the Constitution: A Legal Analysis of the Supreme Court Ruling in Lawrence v. Texas*, by Jody Feder.

[45] *Lawrence v. Texas*, 539 U.S. 558 (2003).

[46] *Id.* at 2484. See e.g., *Wilson v. Ake*, 354 F. Supp.2d at 1306 (declining to interpret Lawrence as creating a fundamental right to same-sex marriage).

[47] As the discussion of state courts' reasoning on this issue, discussed below, indicates, state constitutions – not the U.S. Constitution – are generally the source of interpreting laws governing marriage. To date, only the Arizona Court of Appeals has considered the impact of *Lawrence*. Even then, it did not interpret the case as proscribing state law banning same-sex marriage.

[48] See H.Rept. 104-664, 1996 U.S.C.C.A.N. 2905 (stating that "marriage licensure is not a judgment."). See also, 28 U.S.C. § 1738 (defining which acts, records and judicial proceedings are afforded full faith and credit).

[49] *Restatement (Second) of Conflict of Laws* § 107.

[50] On the state level, common examples of nonnegotiable marital rights and obligations include distinct income tax filing status; public assistance such as health and welfare benefits; default rules concerning community property distribution and control; dower, curtesy and inheritance rights; child custody, child agreements; name change rights; spouse and marital communications privileges in legal proceedings; and the right to bring wrongful death, and other legal actions.

[51] See 2 Restatement (Second) of Conflict of Laws § 283.

[52] Conn. Gen Stat. Ann. § 45a-803-4.

[53] Idaho Code § 32-209.

[54] 750 Ill. Comp. Stat. 5/20 1.

[55] Kan. Stat. Ann. § 23-101.

[56] Mo. Rev. Stat. § 45 1.022.

[57] Pa. Stat. Ann. tit. 23 § 1704.

[58] S.C. Code Ann. § 20-1-10.

[59] Tenn. Code Ann. § 36-3-113.

[60] *Loucks v. Standard Oil Co.*, 120 N.E. 198, 202 (N.Y. 1918)(defining public policy as a valid reason for closing the forum to suit); see e.g. Shea v. Shea, 63 N.E.2d 113 (N.Y. 1945)(finding that a common law marriage validly contracted in another state should not be recognized in New York, where common law marriage was prohibited by statute).

[61] It should be noted that, prior to the *Goodridge* case, in *Adoption of Tammy*, 619 N.E. 2d 315 (Mass. 1993), the Supreme Judicial Court had interpreted "marriage" to mean "the union of one man and one woman."

[62] *Hillary Goodridge v. Dept. of Public Health*, 14 Mass. L. Rptr. 591 (Suffolk County, Super. Ct. May 7, 2002).

[63] *Id.*

[64] *Id.*

[65] *Id.*

[66] *Hillary Goodridge v. Dept. of Public Health*, 798 N.E.2d 941 (Mass. 2003).

[67] *Id.* at 964 (stating that it "cannot be rational under our laws, and indeed is not permitted, to penalize children by depriving them of state benefits because the state disapproves of their parents' sexual orientation.")

[68] *Id.* at 965.

[69] *Id.* at 968.

[70] The state Senate asked the court whether it would be sufficient for the legislature to pass a law allowing same-sex civil unions that would confer "all of the benefits, protections, rights and responsibilities of marriage."

[71] Opinions of the Justices to the Senate, SJC-01963, 802 N.E.2d 565 (Mass. 2004).

[72] As these decisions are based exclusively on state constitutional provisions, they are non-reviewable by the United States Supreme Court.

[73] See, *Kerrigan v. Commissioner of Public Health*, 957 A.2d 407, 412 (Conn. 2008)(stating "... because the institution of marriage carries with it a status and significance that the newly created classification of civil unions does not embody, the segregation of heterosexual and homosexual couples into separate institutions constitutes a cognizable harm.").

[74] *In re Marriage Cases*, 183 P.3d 384 (2008).

[75] *Kerrigan v. Commissioner of Public Health*, 957 A.2d 407 (Conn. 2008); Varnum v. Brien, No. 07-1499, 2009 WL 874044, *30 (Iowa Apr. 3, 2009)(stating " ... a new distinction based on sexual orientation would be equally suspect and difficult to square with the fundamental principles of equal protection embodied in our constitution.").

[76] *See*, 183 P.3d 384, 407-410 (discussing the legislative history of marriage statutes).

[77] *Id.* at 399.

[78] *Id.* at 423.

[79] *Id.*

[80] *Id.*

[81] *Id.*

[82] *Id.* at 433.

[83] Under the federal law, classification or discrimination based on gender is subject to intermediate scrutiny as opposed to strict scrutiny. However, California courts have employed strict scrutiny analysis, thus guaranteeing greater protection against gender discrimination. For example, in *Woods v. Horton*, the court employed a strict scrutiny analysis in finding unconstitutional a state statute that funded certain domestic violence programs only for female victims and their children. 84 Cal.Rptr. 3d 332 (Cal. App. 3 Dist. October 14, 2008).

[84] *See*, 183 P.3d 384, 444 (rejecting the argument that a group's current political powerlessness is a prerequisite in the classification of "suspect" class by stating that "it would be impossible to justify the numerous decisions that continue to treat sex, race, and religion as suspect classifications.").

[85] *Strauss v. Horton*, No. S168047/S168066/S168078 (Ca. Nov. 19, 2008).

[86] *Strauss v. Horton*, 2009 WL 1444594 (Ca. May 26, 2009). Under the California constitution, the initiative process may be used to propose and adopt constitutional amendments but may not be used to revise the state constitution.

[87] *Id.* at *4.

[88] *Id.*

[89] As noted earlier in this chapter, the court concluded that Proposition 8 as a constitutional amendment merely defined the term "marriage" as officially used within the state and, therefore, did not fundamentally alter "a same-sex couple's ... right to establish an officially recognized and protected family relationship." *Id.*

[90] *Id.* at *61.

[91] In the aftermath of *Strauss*, at least one complaint has been filed in district court seeking declaratory and injunctive relief alleging that Proposition 8 is unconstitutional under the Due Process and Equal Protection Clauses of the 14th Amendment of the U.S. Constitution.

[92] It was also a matter of first impression for the Connecticut court to classify sexual orientation as a quasi-suspect class.

[93] *Kerrigan v. Commissioner of Public Health*, 957 A.2d 407, 425 (Conn. 2008).

[94] *Id.* at 473; *Varnum v. Brien*, 2009 WL 874044, *21 (April 3, 2009).

[95] *Lewis v. Harris*, 908 A.2d 196 (NJ 2006) (stating that "the name to be given to the statutory scheme that provides full rights and benefits to same-sex couples, whether marriage or some other term, is a matter left to the democratic process."). As this decision is based solely on New Jersey's state constitution, it is not reviewable by the U.S. Supreme Court.

[96] This was an unanimous decision as to providing benefits and protections to same-sex couples. The dissent concurred in granting benefits and protections but dissented in that they believed that the name "marriage" was also required. *Id.*

[97] *Id.* at 212.

[98] *Id.* at 215.

[99] *Id.*

[100] *Id.* at 218 (stating that "in light of the policies reflected in the statutory and decisional laws of the state, we cannot find a legitimate public need for an unequal legal scheme of benefits and privileges that disadvantages committed same-sex couples.").

[101] *Id.* at 217.

[102] *Id.* at 206.

[103] *Id.* at 223.

[104] *Id.* The New Jersey legislature passed a civil union bill on December 15, 2006, which became effective February 2007.

[105] The Maryland Supreme Court recently ruled that limiting marriage to a man and a woman does not discriminate against gay couples or deny them constitutional rights. In addition, the court stated that the state's prohibition on same- sex marriage promotes the state's interest in heterosexual marriage as a means of having and protecting children. *Conaway v. Deane*, 932 A.2d 571 (MD 2007). Similar results have occurred in New York and Washington. See, *Hernandez v. Robles*, 855 N.E.2d 1 (N.Y. 2006); *Anderson v. King County*, 138 P.3d 963 (Wash. 2006). There are approximately 20 lawsuits filed that seek same-sex marriage rights under state constitutions. These states include California, Connecticut, Florida, Indiana, Nebraska, and Oregon.

[106] *Standhardt v. Superior Court of the State of Arizona*, 77 P.3d 451 (Ariz. Ct. App. 2003).

[107] *Id.* at 457.

[108] *Id.*

[109] *See* also, *Morrison v. Sadler*, 2003 WL 23119998 (Ind. Super. May 7, 2003)(holding that the state's law "promotes the state's interest in encouraging procreation to occur in a context where both biological parents are present to raise the child."); *Lewis v. Harris*, 2003 WL 23191114 (N.J. Super.L. November 5, 2003)(holding that the right to marry does not include a fundamental right to same-sex marriage).

[110] 2005 Ala. Acts 35.

[111] AR. CONST. Amend. 83, sec. 1.

[112] A.Z. CONST. Art. 30.

[113] CA CONST. Art. 1, §7.5.

[114] CO. CONST. Art. II, sec. 31.

[115] FLA CONST. Art. I.

[116] GA. CONST. Art. I., §IV. On May 16, 2006, a state county court stuck down Georgia's constitutional amendment on the grounds that it violated a rule that limits ballot questions to a single subject. *O'Kelley, et. al v. Perdue*, 2004CV93494 (Super. Ct. Fulton County, GA May 16, 2006).

[117] ID CONST. Art. III, § 28.

[118] KS CONST. Art. 15, § 16.

[119] KY. CONST. § 233A.

[120] LA. CONST. Art. XII, §15. The Louisiana Supreme Court reversed a state district judge's ruling striking down the amendment on the grounds that it violated a provision of the state constitution requiring that an amendment cover only one subject. The Court found that each provision of the amendment is germane to the single object of defense of marriage and constitutes an element of the plan advanced to achieve this object. *Forum for Equality PAC v. McKeithen*, 893 So. 2d 715 (La., 2005).

[121] Mi CONST., Art. 1, Sec. 25.

[122] MISS. CONST. §263-A.

[123] MO. CONST., Art. I, Sect. 33.

[124] OKLA. CONST. Art. II, §35.
[125] OR. CONST. Art. XV, §5a.
[126] SC CONST. Art. XVII, §15.
[127] SD CONST. Art. XXI, §9.
[128] TN CONST. Art. XI, §3.
[129] TX CONST. Art. 1, §32.
[130] UTAH CONST. Art. I, §29.
[131] VA CONST. Art. I, §15-A.
[132] WI CONST. Art. XIII, §3.
[133] *See Salucco v. Alldredge*, 17 Mass. L. Rptr. 498 (Mass. Super., 2004)(exercising its general equity jurisdiction to dissolve a Vermont civil union).
[134] *See Langan v. St. Vincent Hosp.*, 196 Misc.2d 440 (N.Y. Misc. 2003)(finding that New York's statutes did not prohibit recognition of a same-sex union nor was such a union against New York's public policy on marriage thus recognizing the same-sex partner as a spouse for purposes of New York's wrongful death statute), overruled by *Langan v. St. Vincent Hosp.*, 802 N.Y.S. 2d 476 (NY AD 2 Dept., 2005).
[135] Constitutional amendments approved in Arkansas, Georgia, Kansas, Kentucky, Michigan, North Dakota, Oklahoma, Ohio and Utah contain language which state that a legal status which is substantially similar to marriage (i.e., civil unions or domestic partnerships) may not be recognized.
[136] On April 7, 2009, Vermont state legislators overrode the governor's veto of a bill legalizing same-sex marriage. It is unclear as to whether civil unions will remain available to same-sex couples.
[137] Vt. Stat. Ann. Tit. 15 §§ 1203, 5163. See also, "The Vermont Guide to Civil Unions," found at http://www.sec.state.vt.us/otherprg/civilunions/civilunions.html.
[138] Vt. Stat. Ann. Tit. 15 § 1204. See also, *Salucco v. Alldredge*, 17 Mass. L. Rptr. 498 (Mass. Super., 2004)(discussing Vermont's civil union statutes).
[139] Connecticut's civil union laws became effective October 1, 2005. A Connecticut civil union is available to an individual at least 18 years of age, of the same sex as the other party to the civil union, no more closely related to the other than first cousin and not a party to another civil union or marriage. 2005 Conn. Legis. Serv. P.A. 05-10 (S.S.B. 963).
[140] New Hampshire's civil union laws became effective January 1, 2008. A New Hampshire civil union is available to an individual at least 18 years of age, of the same sex as the other party to the civil union, no more closely related to the other than first cousin and not a party to another civil union or marriage. N.H. Rev. Stat. §§ 457-A:2-4.
[141] New Jersey's civil union laws became effective February 2007.
[142] CA Fam. §§ 297, 298 and 299(extending the rights and duties of marriage to persons registered as domestic partners on and after January 1, 2005). It should be noted that opposite-sex domestic partners over the age of 62 meeting the eligibility requirements of Title II of the Social Security Act (SSA) for old age benefits (as defined in 42 U.S.C. § 402(a)), or Title XVI of the SSA for aged individuals (as defined in 42 U.S.C. § 1381) are eligible to register as domestic partners.
[143] Hawaii's term for domestic partners is "reciprocal beneficiaries." Reciprocal beneficiaries must be eighteen years old, ineligible to marry, and unmarried. This status includes relationships not involving sex or the same residence. Haw. Rev. Stat. § 572C-5; See also, http://www.hawaii.gov/health (discussing Hawaii's reciprocal beneficiary status).
[144] The New Jersey Domestic Partnership Act became effective July 11, 2004, and grants legal status to same-sex couples and unmarried, opposite-sex couples age 62 or over under certain New Jersey laws.
[145] Oregon's domestic partnership laws went into effect on January 1, 2008.
[146] Washington's domestic partnership laws went into effect on July 22, 2007.
[147] Domestic partnerships also exist at the local level. For example, New York City allows residents an opportunity to register their domestic partnerships provided that both

individuals are eighteen years of age or older, unmarried or related by blood in a manner that would bar his or her marriage in New York State, have a close and committed personal relationship, live together and have been living together on a continuous basis. N.Y.C. Admin. Code § 3-24 1. It should be noted that this statute allows both same-sex and opposite-sex partners to register.

148 H.J.Res. 22 was introduced in the 110th Congress. S.J.Res. 1, S.J.Res. 13, H.J.Res. 39 and H.J.Res. 91 were introduced in the 109th Congress. On June 7, 2006, the Senate considered and voted on a required procedural motion regarding S.J.Res. 1. This motion failed by a vote of 49-48, which prevented further consideration of S.J.Res. 1. In addition, H.J.Res. 56, S.J.Res. 26, S.J.Res. 30, S.J.Res. 40, and H.J.Res. 106 were introduced in the 108th Congress. On July 14, 2004, the Senate considered and voted on a required procedural motion. This motion failed by a vote of 48-50, which prevented further consideration of S.J.Res. 40. On September 30, 2004, the House failed to pass H.J.Res. 106 by a vote of 227-186.

149 H.R. 107 was introduced on January 4, 2007.

150 H.R. 724 is identical to H.R. 3313, the Marriage Protection Act of 2004, introduced during the 108th Congress. On July 22, 2004, the House voted on and passed H.R. 3313. The Senate did not consider the legislation during the 108th Congress. H.R. 1100 was introduced in the 109th Congress and contained the same language.

151 The proposed constitutional amendment would have to be ratified by three-quarters of the states (either the legislatures thereof, or in amendment conventions).

152 It appears that the Netherlands, Belgium, Canada, South Africa, Norway, and Spain are the only international jurisdictions that sanction and/or recognize a same-sex union as a "marriage," per se.

153 Julie A. Greenberg, Defining Male and Female: Intersexuality and the Collision Between Law and Biology, 41 Ariz. L. Rev. 265,309 (1999) (discussing biological characteristics and sexual identity).

154 See e.g., *In re Estate of Gardiner*, 42 P.3d 120 (Kan. 2002); Littleton v. Prange, 9 S.W. 3d 223 (Tex. App. 1999); but see, *M.T. v. J.T.*, 355 A.2d 204 (N.J. 1976)(determining an individual's sexual classification for the purpose of marriage encompasses a mental component as well as an anatomical component).

155 If a mistake was made on the original birth certificate, an amended certificate will sometimes be issued if accompanied by an affidavit from a physician or a court order.

156 It should be noted that only on five occasions previous to the DOMA has Congress enacted legislation based upon this power. The first, passed in 1790 (1 Stat. 122, codified at 28 U.S.C. § 1738), provides for ways to authenticate acts, records and judicial proceedings. The second, dating from 1804 (2 Stat. 298, codified at 28 U.S.C. 1738), provides methods of authenticating non-judicial records. Three other Congressional enactments pertain to modifiable family law orders (child custody, 28 U.S.C. § 1738A, child support (28 U.S.C. § 1738B) and domestic protection (18 U.S.C. § 2265)).

In: Same-Sex Issues
Editors: Jason V. Albertson

ISBN: 978-1-61668-220-0

Chapter 4

HOMOSEXUALS AND THE U.S. MILITARY: CURRENT ISSUES

David F. Burrelli[1] and Jody Feder[2]
[1] Military Manpower Policy
[2] Legislative Attorney

SUMMARY

In 1993, new laws and regulations pertaining to homosexuals and U.S. military service came into effect reflecting a compromise in policy. This compromise, colloquially referred to as "don't ask, don't tell," holds that the presence in the armed forces of persons who demonstrate a propensity or intent to engage in homosexual acts would create an unacceptable risk to the high standards of morale, good order and discipline, and unit cohesion which are the essence of military capability. Service members are not to be asked about nor allowed to discuss their homosexuality. This compromise notwithstanding, the issue has remained politically contentious.

Prior to the 1993 compromise, the number of individuals discharged for homosexuality was generally declining. Since that time, the number of discharges for homosexual conduct has generally increased until recently.

Constitutional challenges to the former and current military policies regarding homosexuals followed in the wake of the new 1993 laws and regulations. Based on the U.S. Supreme Court ruling in *Bowers v. Hardwick* that there is no fundamental right to engage in consensual homosexual sodomy, the courts have uniformly held that the military may discharge a service member for overt homosexual conduct. However, the legal picture was complicated by the Court's 2003 decision in *Lawrence v. Texas* which overruled *Bowers* by declaring unconstitutional a Texas law that prohibited sexual acts between same sex couples. In addition, unsettled legal questions remain as to whether a discharge based solely on a statement that a service member is homosexual transgresses constitutional limits. Meanwhile, efforts to allow individuals of the same sex to marry legally appear unlikely to affect the Department of Defense (DOD) policy in the near term, since such individuals are barred from serving in the military, although court challenges are possible.

In addition, many academic institutions have enacted rules that protect homosexuals from discrimination on campus. As a result, colleges, universities, and even high schools have sought to bar military recruiters from their campuses and/or to eliminate Reserve Officer Training Corps (ROTC) programs on campus because of the DOD policy on homosexuals in the military. At the same time, legislation has been enacted that bars giving federal funds to campuses that block access for military recruiters. On March 6, 2006, the Supreme Court reversed a federal appeals court ruling in *Rumsfeld v. Forum for Academic and Institutional Rights (FAIR),* and upheld the constitutionality of the Solomon Amendment, which prohibits certain federal funding to higher educational institutions that deny access by military recruiters to their students equal to that provided to other employers.

In recent years, several members of Congress have expressed interest in amending "don't ask, don't tell." At least one bill that would repeal the law and replace it with a policy of nondiscrimination on the basis of sexual orientation—H.R. 1 283—has been introduced in the 111th Congress.

BACKGROUND AND ANALYSIS

Early in the 1992 presidential campaign, then-candidate Bill Clinton commented that, if elected, he would "lift the ban" on homosexuals serving in the military.[1] Existing policies had been in place since the Carter Administration and, historically speaking, homosexuality had not been tolerated in the military services. The issue drew heated debate among policymakers and the public at large. In response to congressional concerns,

President Clinton put into place in early 1993, an interim compromise that allowed the Department of Defense (DOD) an opportunity to study the issue and develop a "draft executive order" that would end discrimination on the basis of "sexual orientation." This interim compromise (announced on January 29, 1993) also provided Congress additional time to more fully exercise its constitutional authority under Article I, Section 8, clause 14, "To make rules for the Government and Regulation of the land and naval Forces," including the consideration of legislation and the holding of hearings on the issue. In announcing the interim agreement, the President noted that the Joint Chiefs of Staff agreed to remove questions regarding sexual orientation from the enlistment application.[2] One of the elements of the compromise was an agreement within the Congress not to immediately enact legislation that would have maintained the prior policy (of barring homosexuals from service and continuing to ask recruits questions concerning their sexuality) until after the completion of a congressional review.[3]

The Senate and House Armed Services Committees (SASC and HASC) held extensive hearings on the issue in 1993. By May 1993, a congressional consensus appeared to emerge over what then-SASC chairman Sam Nunn described as a "don't ask, don't tell" approach. Under this approach, DOD would not ask questions concerning the sexual orientation of prospective members of the military, and individuals would be required to either keep their homosexual orientation to themselves, or, if they did not, they would be discharged if already in the service or denied enlistment/appointment if seeking to join the service.

On July 19, 1993, President Clinton announced his new policy on homosexuals in the military. According to the President, the policy was to be made up of these essential elements:

> One, service men and women will be judged based on their conduct, not their sexual orientation. Two, therefore the practice ..., of not asking about sexual orientation in the enlistment procedure will continue. Three, an open statement by a service member that he or she is a homosexual will create a rebuttable presumption that he or she intends to engage in prohibited conduct, but the service member will be given an opportunity to refute that presumption;.... And four, all provisions of the Uniform Code of Military Justice will be enforced in an even-handed manner as regards both heterosexuals and homosexuals. And thanks to the policy provisions agreed to by the Joint Chiefs, there will be a decent regard to the legitimate privacy and associational rights of all service members.[4]

The Administration dubbed this policy, "don't ask, don't tell, don't pursue." It is noteworthy that the President did not mention "don't pursue" in the announcement of the policy on July 19, 1993. The inclusion of "don't pursue" (akin to a "don't investigate" stance advocated by homosexual rights groups) seemingly created a contradiction in the President's policy.[5] On the one hand, it maintained the notion of military necessity and privacy as found in the congressional compromise of "don't ask, don't tell," and then appeared to prevent efforts to enforce the regulations and laws which implement the broad policy by limiting the military's role via "don't pursue." This problem was discussed at hearings with then-Secretary of Defense Les Aspin. Secretary Aspin indicated that individuals could acknowledge their homosexuality without risking an investigation or discharge;[6] later he said that individual statements might not be credible grounds for investigating if the commander so decided, but, if investigated, such statements could be credible grounds for a discharge proceeding. Ultimately, the Secretary agreed that statements are grounds for investigations and possible discharge.

In these same hearings, held from March 29, 1993 through July 22, 1993, Senators raised numerous questions as to what behavior, if any, would justify the commencement of an investigation, and what grounds would justify an administrative discharge.[7] Since commanders and noncommissioned officers are not usually lawyers, many critics argued that such rules created legal technicalities that would prove dysfunctional in a military setting, and/or lead to an expansion of unpredictable court remedies.[8] At the same time, some argued that this outcome would not have displeased the Administration, even if it was not the original intent. This thesis held that implementation of the compromise policy would have encouraged judicial intervention and, thereby, would have provided a means to seek a judicial resolution asserting that the compromise was unconstitutional. These critics hypothesized that the Clinton Administration may have been following a strategy of tacitly implementing a muddled regulation, awaiting a legal challenge, then poorly defending the policy—thereby encouraging judicial intervention in finding the policy unconstitutional.[9] Administration officials insisted that the President was merely trying to pursue a compromise that would take into account the concerns of the Congress and the military, but would also minimize discrimination against homosexuals. [10]

The policy announced by the Clinton Administration was based in large part, on sexual "orientation."[11] This term has generated problems concerning its practical definition. Some view a sexual "orientation" as non-behavioral while others do not exclude behavioral manifestations when speaking of a sexual "orientation." As will be discussed below, the Clinton Administration's use of the term was subject to varying interpretations.

The ambiguities in the Administration's interpretation of the policy, as well as conflicting legal rulings at the time, seemingly encouraged Congress to act. On November 30, 1993, the FY1994 National Defense Authorization Act was signed into law by President Clinton (P.L. 103-160). Section 571 of the law, codified at 10 United States Code 654, describes homosexuality in the ranks as an "unacceptable risk ... to morale, good order, and discipline." The law codified the grounds for discharge as follows: (1) the member has engaged in, attempted to engage in, or solicited another to engage in a homosexual act or acts; (2) the member states that he or she is a homosexual or bisexual; or (3) the member has married or attempted to marry someone of the same sex. The law also stated that DOD would brief new entrants (accessions) and members about the law and policy on a regular basis. Finally, the law instructed that asking questions of new recruits concerning sexuality could be resumed—having been halted in January, 1993—on a discretionary basis. As such, this law represented a discretionary don't ask, definitely don't tell policy. Notably, the law contains no mention of "orientation." In many ways, this law contained a reiteration of the basic thrust of the pre-1993 policy (although it does not mention any restrictions regarding 'asking' about a person's sexuality).

On December 22, 1993, Secretary of Defense Aspin released new DOD regulations to implement the statute enacted the preceding month. Language in these regulations indicated that the Secretary was trying to incorporate both the restrictions in the law, and the President's desire to open military service "to those who have a homosexual orientation." The policy stated:

> A Service member may also be separated if he or she states that he or she is a homosexual or bisexual, or words to that effect. Such a statement creates a rebuttable presumption that the member engages in homosexual acts or has a propensity or intent to do so. The Service member will have the opportunity to rebut that presumption, however, by demonstrating that he or she does not engage in homosexual acts and does not have a propensity or intent to do so.[12]

However, the policy—not the law it ostensibly implemented—stated that "sexual orientation is considered a personal and private matter, and homosexual orientation is not a bar to service entry or continued service unless manifested by homosexual conduct." According to this statement of DOD regulations, "sexual orientation" was defined as "A sexual attraction to individuals of a particular sex." Following Aspin's resignation and the confirmation of William Perry as the new Secretary of Defense in February 1994, DOD reportedly accepted the recommendation of certain Senators to delete from DOD regulations the phrase, "homosexual orientation ... is not a bar to military service."[13] In its place, DOD inserted the statement:

> A person's sexual orientation is considered a personal and private matter, and is not a bar to service or continued service unless manifested by homosexual conduct ...[14]

In addition, the definition of "sexual orientation" was modified:

> An abstract sexual preference for persons of a particular sex, as distinct from a propensity or intent to engage in sexual acts.[15]

The elusiveness of the definition of "orientation" is apparent. Under the Administration's original definition, "orientation" is a sexual attraction. Under the revised definition, it is an abstract preference. Other sources define sexual "orientation" to include overt sexual behavior.[16]

Current regulations, therefore, are based on conduct, including verbal or written statements. Since sexual "orientation" is "personal and private," DOD is not to ask and personnel are not to tell. Should an individual choose to make his or her homosexual "orientation" public—i.e., no longer private and personal, nor abstract—an investigation and discharge may well occur.

The ambiguous nature of the term "orientation" and its usage has not been without problems. In 1994, a Navy tribunal decided not to discharge Lt. Maria Zoe Dunning after she had made the statement "I am a lesbian" at a January 1993 rally. Her attorneys argued that she was not broadcasting her intentions to practice homosexuality but merely acknowledging her "sexual orientation." In the view of the reviewing officers, she had successfully rebutted the presumption that she would commit homosexual acts. Such a finding, if not inconsistent with the law and regulations, created a legal avenue via which homosexuals could announce their sexuality without being discharged. Shortly afterward, the Department of Defense Office of the General Counsel released a memo,[17] in August 1995, addressing this issue:

> A member may not avoid the burden of rebutting the presumption merely by asserting that his or her statement of homosexuality was intended

> to convey only a message about sexual orientation ..., and not to convey any message about propensity or intent to engage in homosexual acts. To the contrary, by virtue of the statement, the member bears the burden of proof that he or she does not engage in, and does not attempt, have a propensity, [n]or intend to engage in homosexual acts. If the member in rebuttal offers evidence that he or she does not engage in homosexual acts or have a propensity or intent to do so, the offering of the evidence does not shift the burden of proof to the government. Rather, the burden of proof remains on the member throughout the proceeding.[18]

As written, the law makes no mention of sexual "orientation," and is structured entirely around the concept of sexual "conduct" including statements concerning an individual's sexuality. Therefore, attempts to implement the statute, or analyze and evaluate it, in terms of "sexual orientation," have resulted in confusion and ambiguity, and are likely to continue to do so.

In recent years, several members of Congress have expressed interest in amending "don't ask, don't tell," and at least one bill that would repeal the law and replace it with a policy of nondiscrimination on the basis of sexual orientation—H.R. 1 283—has been introduced in the 111th Congress. In addition, Senator Gillibrand was reportedly planning to introduce an amendment to the National Defense Authorization Act (H.R. 2647/S. 1390) that would have temporarily prohibited DOD from initiating investigations or discharges pursuant to "don't ask, don't tell," but, according to news reports, the Senator has reconsidered and has adopted a waitand-see approach with regard to amending "don't ask, don't tell."[19]

DISCHARGE STATISTICS

Reports in the media over the last several years have stated that since the implementation of the "don't ask, don't tell" policy in 1993, the number of discharges for homosexuality has increased.[20] According to data provided by DOD and reproduced in **Table 1** from the early 1980s until Fiscal Year (FY) 1994, the number of personnel discharged for homosexual conduct (including statements) decreased. From FY1995 to FY2001, the numbers rebounded, only to begin leveling off thereafter.

In April 1998, the Department of Defense released a review of the implementation of the "Policy on Homosexual Conduct." This review was instituted after complaints were aired that the increasing rate of discharges was a sign of "witch hunts" or anti-homosexual harassment. In its review, DOD concluded that "for the most part, the policy has been properly applied and enforced." DOD also stated:

> First, we found that the large majority of the discharges for homosexual conduct are based on the statements of service members who identify themselves as homosexual, as opposed to cases involving homosexual acts. The services believe that most of these statements— although not all of them—involve service members who voluntarily elect to disclose their sexual orientation to their peers, supervisors or commanders. The increase in the number of discharges for homosexual conduct since 1994 is attributable to this increase in statement cases. Discharges for homosexual acts and marriages has declined by 20% over the past three years [1994-1997]. Second, most of those discharged under the policy are junior personnel with very little time in the military, and most of the increase in discharges for homosexual conduct has occurred in this sector. The number of cases involving career service members is relatively small. Third, the great majority of discharges for homosexual conduct are uncontested and are processed administratively. Finally, more than 98% of all members discharged in Fiscal Year 1997 under the policy received honorable discharges. (Separation of enlisted members in their first 180 days of military service are generally uncharacterized.) Discharges under other than honorable conditions or courts-martial for consensual homosexual conduct are infrequent and have invariably involved aggravating circumstances or additional charges.[21]

With over a decade (1993-2008) of experience under the most recent changes instituted during the Clinton Administration, other explanations as to why individuals may announce their homosexuality have come forward. Most notable is the observation that the vast majority of those discharged for homosexuality are discharged because they made voluntary statements identifying themselves as homosexual, bisexual or having such an "orientation." Some have speculated recently that these statements are made by service members so as to enable them to terminate their military obligations before their term of service is completed regardless of their sexual "orientation."[22]

Advocacy groups have claimed that anti-homosexual harassment has increased since the 1998 review, and that those discharges were brought about by "witch hunts," or invasive and unwarranted searching and discharging of homosexuals in the ranks.[23] Although cases of aggressive investigations have been reported, the data would not appear to support the general use of such tactics. Recently, as the number of discharges has decreased, activists claim the Administration is retaining homosexuals because of the need for manpower as a result of Operations Enduring Freedom and Iraqi Freedom. At the same time, activists bemoan the discharge of a number of linguists who were found to be homosexuals.[24] Critics contend that the activists are trying to have it both ways when "analyzing" data. From the data, it can be seen that homosexuals who are discharged represent an extremely small percentage of the force. For instance, if it is assumed that homosexuals make up only 1.6% of the total active force of approximately 1.4 million,[25] there would be an estimated 22,400 homosexuals in uniform. In 2003, 653 or 2.9% of the estimated homosexuals in uniform were discharged for homosexual conduct.

Some have claimed that discharges decline during time of war, suggesting that the military ignores homosexuality when soldiers are most needed, only to "kick them out" once the crisis has passed.[26] It is notable that during wartime, the military services can, and have, instituted actions "to suspend certain laws relating to ... separation" that can limit administrative discharges. These actions, known as "stop-loss,"[27] allow the services to minimize the disruptive effects of personnel turnover during a crisis. However, administrative discharges for homosexual conduct normally are *not* affected by stop-loss. It can be speculated that a claim of homosexuality during a crisis may be viewed skeptically, but under the policy would require an investigation. Stop-loss, as implemented requires an investigation to determine if the claim is bona fide or being used for some other reason, such as avoiding deployment overseas and/or to a combat zone. If, following an investigation, such a claim were found to be in violation of the law on homosexual conduct, the services could not use "stop-loss" to delay an administrative discharge.[28]

In practice, it is quite possible for an individual, during a crisis, to claim to be a homosexual and to be deployed while awaiting the results of an investigation. Likewise, a claim made during a non-crisis situation would more likely be dealt with in a routine manner, leading to a discharge. Homosexual rights groups assert that commanders tend to be more reluctant to discharge someone during a crisis situation. They contend that differing treatment of gays during crisis and non-crisis situation creates a double standard. Likewise, commanders and others are often more skeptical of such claims made during a crisis.

According to an Army Reserve Component Unit Commander's Handbook,[29] homosexual conduct is one of many criteria necessitating "personnel action during the mobilization process...." According to this document, if a discharge for homosexuality "has been requested and approved prior to the unit's receipt of alert notification, the member will be discharged prior to the unit's effective date of [active duty]." Further, if "discharge is requested but not yet approved, delayed entry will be requested ... pending final determination." Finally, if "discharge is not requested prior to the unit's receipt of alert notification, discharge is not authorized."

Some homosexual activists claim that this is proof that the military retains known homosexuals during a time of crisis/mobilization. This language addresses the possibility of a false claim of homosexuality being used as a means of avoiding a mobilization. If such a claim is made, an investigation is likely to occur. If the claim is false, the individual would be retained (and possibly disciplined for making a false claim). If the claim is found to be true, a discharge would be in order. Retaining individuals who violate the rules pertaining to homosexuals in uniform is a violation of federal law.

Listed in **Table 1** are the homosexual discharge statistics from FY1980 to FY2008. In January 1981, the then-current policy on administrative discharges for homosexuality was reinstituted under new wording to allow for the continuation of homosexual discharges while addressing legal concerns over the wording of the previous policy.[30] The active duty force numbered approximately 2.1 million throughout the 1980s. By FY2000, active duty personnel numbers fell to a then low of 1,384,338. The numbers increased to 1,434,377 in FY2004 and seemed to level off thereafter. Because of this drop in manpower levels, it is important to consider not just the number of homosexual discharges in any particular year, but the changes in discharges as a percentage of the total active force.

The data in **Table 1** show the percentage of discharges fell from FY1982 to FY1994. The percentage of discharges rose from FY1994 to FY2001. In FY2001, the number/percentage discharged was smaller than the previous peak of FY1982. Since FY2001, the numbers/percentages have begun to decline and later level off. These percentages were declining prior to, and continued to decline following the 1991 Persian Gulf War (Operations Desert Shield/Desert Storm). If, as some have speculated, DOD was using "Stop Loss" to retain homosexuals during that war, we would have expected to see a drop in the wartime discharge rate followed by an increase following the crisis. Such a pattern is not evident in these data.

During the period covered by these data, the average percentage discharged was 0.063%. For the period prior to the implementation of the new policy (and law), i.e. FY1980 to FY1992, the average percentage discharged was 0.068%. For the period FY1993 to FY2008, the average was 0.059%. The difference in the percentage discharged before and following the implementation of the new policy was statistically insignificant. Thus, although the data appear to move in differing directions prior to and following the implementation of the new policy, statistical analysis suggests that such changes may reflect random fluctuations in the data.[31]

Table 1. Homosexual Conduct Administrative Separation Discharge Statistics

Fiscal Year	Total Number of Homosexual Discharges	Percentage of Total Active Force
1980	1,754	0.086
1981	1,817	0.088
1982	1,998	0.095
1983	1,815	0.085
1984	1,822	0.085
1985	1,660	0.077
1986	1,643	0.076
1987	1,380	0.063
1988	1,101	0.051
1989	996	0.047
1990	941	0.046
1991	949	0.048
1992	730	0.040
1993	682	0.040
1994	617	0.038
1995	757	0.050
1996	858	0.058
1997	997	0.069
1998	1,145	0.081
1999	1,034	0.075
2000	1,212	0.088
2001	1,227	0.089
2002	885	0.063
2003	770	0.054
2004	653	0.046

Table 1. (Continued)

Fiscal Year	Total Number of Homosexual Discharges	Percentage of Total Active Force
2005	726	0.052
2006	612	0.044
2007	635	0.046
2008	634	0.045

Sources: Data for the years 1980 through 1997 are from U.S. Department of Defense, Office of the Assistant Secretary of Defense (Personnel and Readiness), Report to the Secretary of Defense, *Review of the Effectiveness of the Application and Enforcement of the Department's Policy on Homosexual Conduct in the Military*, April 1998. Percentages may vary slightly due to rounding. Data for later years are from the Department of Defense, Defense Manpower Data Center. Year 2005 data are from Files, John, "Military's discharges for being gay rose in '05," *New York Times*, August 15, 2006. Data from 2006-2008 are from DOD office of Legislative Affairs.

ISSUES

Legal Challenges

Constitutional challenges to former and contemporary military policies regarding homosexuals began to accelerate following implementation of the "don't ask, don't tell" compromise in 1993. A lengthy tradition of "special deference" to the political branches led most federal district and appeals courts to affirm the "considered professional judgment" of military leaders to discipline or discharge a service member for homosexual conduct or speech. Based on the 1986 Supreme Court ruling in *Bowers v. Hardwick* that there is no fundamental right to engage in consensual homosexual sodomy,[32] the courts ruled that the military could constitutionally discharge a service member for overt homosexual behavior. Judicial challenges to "don't ask, don't tell" focused on the "statements" provision of the new policy which presumes, absent contrary evidence, homosexual activity or a "propensity" to act on the part of any service member who acknowledges his/her homosexuality.[33] The High Court has refused to review the military's "don't ask, don't tell" policy on several occasions, the last in 1999 when it declined to hear the appeal of two former service members who were discharged after declaring their homosexuality to commanding officers. Without comment, the Justices declined to consider arguments that the policy was based on prejudice against homosexuals and violates their free speech rights.[34]

Complicating the legal picture, however, is the Court's 2003 ruling in *Lawrence v. Texas*,[35] which declared unconstitutional a Texas law that prohibited sexual acts between same sex couples. Justice Kennedy, writing for the majority, held that the "liberty" interest in privacy guaranteed by the due process clause of the Fourteenth Amendment protects a right for adults to engage in private, consensual homosexual conduct. The *Lawrence* majority expressly overruled *Bowers*' contrary conclusion. Justice Kennedy agreed with the dissent in *Bowers* that "[t]he statutes do seek to control a personal relationship that, whether or not entitled to formal recognition in the law, is within the liberty of persons to choose without being punished as criminals." The majority opinion continued:

> The petitioners are entitled to respect for their private lives. The State cannot demean their existence or control their destiny by making their private sexual conduct a crime. The right to liberty under the Due Process Clause gives them the full right to engage in their conduct without the intervention of the government. It is a promise of the Constitution that there is a realm of personal liberty which the government cannot enter. The Texas statute furthers no legitimate state interest which can justify its intrusion into the personal and private life of the individual.[36]

In particular, the community's moral disapproval of homosexuality was no "rational" justification for deploying the power of the state to enforce those views. Justice O'Connor concurred in the judgment, but rather than overrule *Bowers*, would have declared the Texas statute unconstitutional on equal protection grounds because it did not likewise prohibit sodomy between opposite sex couples.

Based on *Bowers,* earlier federal appellate courts uniformly ruled that the military ban on homosexual acts intruded upon no constitutionally protected right and was "rationally related" to legitimate military needs for "unit cohesion" and discipline. Moreover, by equating the admission of homosexuality by individual service members—unless demonstrated otherwise—with "propensity" for illegal conduct, the "don't ask, don't tell" policy successfully avoided equal protection and first amendment challenge as well. After *Lawrence*, however, the constitutional bulwark of *Bowers* has crumbled, arming opponents of Article 125,[37] and "don't ask, don't tell," with an argument that current military policies abridge the due process right to privacy of homosexual service members. But to prevail in that argument, any future challenger may still have to demonstrate that findings by Congress regarding those policies defy minimal rationality, a weighty burden given the deference historically accorded the political branches in the management of military affairs. The precise standard of judicial review, in the wake of *Lawrence*, however, has yet to be firmly established.

A tradition of deference by the courts to Congress and the Executive in the organization and regulation of the military dates from the earliest days of the republic. Motivating development of this constitutional doctrine was the separation of powers among the executive, judicial, and legislative branches. The Constitution grants exclusive authority to raise and support the armed forces to Congress,[38] which has "broad and sweeping" power to make all laws necessary for that purpose.[39] Similarly, the Constitution grants exclusive command of the armed forces to the executive branch, designating the President as "commander-in-chief."[40] Nowhere does the Constitution delineate a specific role for the judiciary in military matters. Judicial authority over the armed forces arises only indirectly as arbiter of constitutional rights. Thus, the policy of extraordinary deference "to the professional judgment of military authorities" has emerged from case law,[41] particularly "when legislative action under the congressional authority to raise and support armies and make rules and regulations for their governance is challenged."[42]

Originally framed as a doctrine of noninterference, the early Court avoided all substantive review of military disciplinary proceedings, provided only that jurisdictional prerequisites were met. A more skeptical judicial attitude emerged during the Warren Court era, which frequently questioned the scope and operation of military rules, particularly as applied to on-base civilians and non-duty-related conduct of service members. But the pendulum returned to what has been described as the " modern military deference doctrine" with a series of Burger Court decisions in the mid-1970s. Rather than abandoning all substantive review, the current judicial approach is to apply federal constitutional standards in a more lenient fashion which, with rare exception, favors military needs for obedience and discipline over the rights of the individual servicemen. "The fundamental necessity for obedience, and the consequent necessity for imposition of discipline, may render permissible within the military that which would be constitutionally impermissible outside it."[43]

Among leading contemporary precedents are the Supreme Court rulings in *Goldman v. Weinberger* and *Rostker v. Goldberg*.[44] Goldman was an Orthodox

Jew and rabbi serving as a commissioned officer and psychologist for the Air Force. For five years, he wore a yarmulke while in uniform, without objection from superiors until he testified as a defense witness in a court martial proceeding. The prosecuting attorney at the court martial complained to Goldman's commanding officer that wearing the yarmulke violated Air Force regulations that prohibited wearing of headgear indoors. Goldman was ultimately separated from the service for refusal to remove the yarmulke.

Goldman argued that the Air Force regulation banning headgear "infringed upon his First Amendment freedom to exercise his religious beliefs." Writing for a five-to-four Supreme Court majority, Justice Rehnquist disagreed:

> Our review of military regulation challenged on First Amendment grounds is far more deferential than constitutional review of similar laws or regulations designed for civilian society. The military need not encourage debate or tolerate protest to the extent that such tolerance is required of the civilian state by the First Amendment; to accomplish its mission the military must foster instinctive obedience, unity, commitment, and esprit de corps. The essence of military service 'is the subordination of the desires and interests of the individual to the needs of the service.'[45]

Because the Air Force argued that standardized uniforms were necessary to "encourage the subordination of personal preferences," the majority deferred to the "professional judgment" of the Air Force. The ramifications of the majority's "subrational-basis standard—absolute, uncritical deference" drew a vigorous dissent from Justice Brennan, and separately from Justice O'Connor who objected:

> The Court rejects Captain Goldman's claim without even the slightest attempt to weigh his asserted right to the free exercise of his religion against the interest of the Air Force in uniformity of dress within the military hospital. No test for free exercise claims in the military context is even articulated, much less applied. It is entirely sufficient for the Court if the military perceives a need for uniformity.[46]

In *Rostker v. Goldberg*,[47] the Supreme Court dealt specifically with an equal protection challenge to gender-based military classifications—namely, Congress' decision to register men, but not women, for the military draft. In applying the "intermediate scrutiny" test of *Craig v. Boren,*[48] the majority found the draft law did not reflect "unthinking" gender stereotypes, but was the product of extensive congressional deliberations on the role of women in combat and the necessities of military mobilization. The purpose of registration was to create a pool from which combat troops could be drawn as needed. Because women were barred from combat by another law, they were not "similarly situated" to men, and their exemption from registration was "not only sufficiently but closely related to" an "important" governmental purpose. As important to the outcome, however, was the Court's articulation of the "healthy deference" due the political branches in managing military affairs. Thus, according to the majority opinion, "[t]he military constitutes a specialized community governed by a separate discipline from that of the civilian," such that "Congress is permitted to legislate both with greater breadth and with greater flexibility when prescribing the rules by which [military society] shall be governed.... " Constitutional rules apply, and may not be disregarded, but "the different character of the military community and of the military mission requires different application of those principles." [49]

Equal deference to the military's judgment was apparent in four federal appeals court rulings to uphold the "don't ask, don't tell" policy before *Lawrence*. First to rule was the Fourth Circuit inan appeal by Lt. Paul G. Thomasson, who had been honorably discharged under the policy after he announced in March 1994 that he was homosexual. Writing for the nine-member majority in *Thomasson v. Perry*,[50] Chief Judge J. Harvie Wilkinson III stressed Congress' "plenary control" of the military and the "deference" owed both the Executive and Legislative Branches in matters of national defense as factors calling for judicial restraint when faced with challenges to military decision making. "What Thomasson challenges," the opinion notes, "is a statute that embodies the exhaustive efforts of the democratically accountable branches of American government and an enactment that reflects month upon month of political negotiation and deliberation." Under this standard, Judge Wilkinson concluded that the government articulated a "legitimate purpose" for excluding individuals who commit homosexual acts—that of maintaining unit cohesion and military readiness—and that the law's rebuttable presumption was a "rational means" of preventing individuals who engage in, or have a "propensity" to engage in, homosexual conduct from serving in the military. Similarly, Thomasson's First Amendment claims were rejected for the reason that:

> [t]he statute does not target speech declaring homosexuality; rather it targets homosexual acts and the propensity or intent to engage in homosexual acts and permissibly uses the speech as evidence. The use of speech as

evidence in this manner does not raise a constitutional issue—the First Amendment does not prohibit the evidentiary use of speech to establish the elements of a crime, or, as is the case here, to prove motive or intent.[51]

Subsequently, the Fourth Circuit relied on *Thomasson* to affirm a ruling by federal District Judge Ellis in *Thorne v. U.S. Department of Defense.*[52] After reviewing the record in eight other administrative separation proceedings where the presumption that a declared homosexual has a propensity to engage in forbidden conduct was successfully rebutted, Judge Ellis in *Thorne* held that conduct rather than speech was the target of the "don't ask, don't tell" policy.

In *Richenberg v. Perry,*[53] the Eighth Circuit upheld the "statement" provision of "don't ask, don't tell" as applied to the discharge of an Air Force captain who had informed his commanding officer that he was homosexual. As in *Thomasson,* the policy was alleged to violate equal protection and free speech rights by targeting declarations of "homosexual orientation or status" unrelated to conduct and for "irrational catering to prejudice against and hatred of homosexuals." Agreeing with the Fourth Circuit, however, the *Richenberg* court found that the policy ban on homosexual acts was justified by legitimate military needs and rationally served by the rebuttable presumption of a "propensity" to act on the part of declared homosexuals. And because the focus of "don't ask, don't tell" is to "identify and exclude those who are likely to engage in homosexual acts," while prohibiting direct inquiries into an applicant's sexual orientation, there was no basis for a First Amendment challenge, the court concluded.

In appeals from three district court rulings during 1997, the Ninth Circuit approved the discharge of a naval petty officer who admitted to sexual relations with other men, *Philips v. Perry,*[54] and of a California National Guardsman and Navy lieutenant who had submitted written documents to their commanding officers acknowledging that they were homosexual.[55] In the former case, the appeals court ruled that homosexuals are not members of a "suspect class" for purposes of federal equal protection analysis, that the military ban on homosexual "acts" was rationally related to legitimate governmental interest in "maintaining effective armed forces," and that evidentiary use of admitted homosexuality did not violate a service member's First Amendment rights. Because sufficient homosexual acts were alleged to justify discharge, the *Perry* court declined considering the constitutionality of the rebuttable presumption and statements prong of the military policy. That issue was revisited in *Holmes* and *Watson*, however, where the Ninth Circuit ruled that military personnel who "tell," without also presenting evidence to rebut the inference that they engage in homosexual acts, may constitutionally be discharged from the service. Writing for a divided three-judge panel, Circuit Judge Wiggins "agree[d] with the Second, Fourth, and Eighth Circuits on this issue. Although the legislature's assumption that declared homosexuals will engage in homosexual conduct is imperfect, it is sufficiently rational to survive [equal protection] scrutiny ... "[56]

In *Able v. United States*,[57] upholding the "don't ask, don't tell" policy, the Second Circuit faulted a contrary federal district judge's decision for failing to give proper deference to Congress and the military judgment. The opinion emphasized a judicial tradition of applying "less stringent standards" of constitutional review to military rules than to laws and regulations governing civilian society. Judicial deference was warranted by the need for discipline and unit cohesion within this "specialized community," matters for which courts "are ill-suited to second-guess military judgments that bear upon military capability and readiness." In addition, "extensive Congressional hearings and deliberation" provided a "rational basis" for the government's contention that the prohibition on homosexual conduct "promotes unit cohesion, enhances privacy and reduces sexual tension." Consequently, the court concluded, "[g]iven the strong presumption of validity we give to classifications under rational basis review and the special respect accorded to Congress' decisions regarding military matters, we will not substitute our judgment for that of Congress."

Some argue that the *Lawrence* ruling in 2003 altered the constitutional framework for analyzing both Article 125 and the "don't ask, don't tell" policy. According to this view, by finding a fundamental liberty interest in consensual homosexual activity, *Lawrence* demands closer scrutiny of both the means and ends of the current military policy. Under traditional equal protection doctrine, the legislature has broad latitude to draw lines based on any "non-suspect" classification—homosexuality included—provided only that the policy is "rationally related" to a "legitimate" governmental interest. In the past, the military has satisfied this "lenient" test by invoking the need for unit cohesion, discipline, and morale—interests uniformly affirmed by pre-*Lawrence* appellate courts to uphold the "don't ask, don't tell" policy. The government generally bears a far greater burden, however, when defending any action that interferes with individual rights or liberty interests deemed "fundamental" for due process purposes. To pass constitutional muster, the challenged measure or policy must be "narrowly tailored" to a "compelling" governmental interest.[58]

In this regard, Article 125 has been criticized by its opponents for codifying the same "moral disapproval" as the Texas statute involved in *Lawrence* and for being over-broad and underinclusive. One commentator stated:

> This broad ban does not limit itself to sodomy on military premises, nor to acts of sodomy between superiors and inferiors in the chain of command ... It is not limited to any context in which one might think there were secondary effects separate from moral disapproval. *Lawrence* tells us that mere disapproval, standing alone, is an inadequate basis for such a law.[59]

Consequently, some argue that military interests in good order and discipline previously accepted by the courts are not sufficient to trump the liberty interest identified by *Lawrence*. Supporters of the continued viability of Article 125 and the "don't ask, don't tell" policy, however, argue that there is no immediate parallel between constitutional precedent as applied to the civilian and military sectors. Thus, the unbroken line of appellate decisions supporting current homosexual policies, aided by the modern military deference doctrine, would as likely tilt the balance in the government's favor in any future judicial contest. Moreover, some argue that whatever implications *Lawrence* may have on Article 125, a penal statute, may not be directly translatable to the "don't ask, don't tell" policy, which provides for administrative separation from the military, but no criminal penalty.

The task of parsing these issues has fallen to the courts as they confront a new generation of legal challenges to the military's homosexual policies. In 2004, for example, the U.S. Court of Appeals for the Armed Forces, which is the military's highest judicial tribunal, issued a decision regarding the appeal of an Air Force linguistic specialist who was convicted by court martial on sex-related charges, including consensual sodomy with a subordinate. That case, *United States v. Marcum*, appears to have established the current standard that military courts use to evaluate post- *Lawrence* challenges to military policies regarding homosexuals.[60] A central issue in the case was whether *Lawrence* nullifies Article 125 and compels reversal of the service-member's sodomy conviction. The appeals court upheld Marcum's conviction, but not strictly on the basis of homosexual activity, instead pointing to the inappropriateness of sex between subordinate and superiors in the same chain of command. In *dicta*, the court strongly suggested that *Lawrence's* ban on laws prohibiting sexual intimacy may apply to the military as well. It even went on to "assume without deciding" that Marcum's conduct did fall within the protections of *Lawrence*. Such protection, however, was insufficient to shield him from the gender-neutral charge of sex with a subordinate.

In reaching its decision, the *Marcum* court established a test that provides guidance on how to apply the principles of *Lawrence* to the military environment. Any challenge to convictions under Article 125 are reviewed on a case-by-case basis according to the following three-part test:

> First, was the conduct that the accused was found guilty of committing of a nature to bring it within the liberty interest identified by the Supreme Court? Second, did the conduct encompass any behavior or factors identified by the Supreme Court as outside the analysis in *Lawrence* [e.g., involving public conduct, minors, prostitutes, or persons who might be injured/coerced or who are situated in relationships where consent might not easily be refused]? Third, are there additional factors relevant solely in the military environment that affect the nature and reach of the *Lawrence* liberty interest?[61]

In the wake of *Marcum*, some courts appear to be skeptical of challenges to Article 125 and "don't ask, don't tell," especially when other factors, such as homosexual activity with a subordinate, are involved. For example, in *Loomis v. United States*, the United States Court of Federal Claims applied the *Marcum* test to the case of a lieutenant who was discharged for homosexual conduct.[62] Because the lieutenant was of significantly higher rank than the private with whom he had had sexual relations, the court found that "the nature of the relationship between plaintiff and the PFC ... is such that consent might not easily be refused and thus it is outside of the liberty interest protected by *Lawrence*."[63] In other cases, however, courts have been more receptive to *Lawrence*-based challenges to military policies regarding homosexuals. For example in *United States v. Bullock*,[64] the U.S. Army Court of Criminal Appeals relied on *Lawrence* to overturn the guilty plea of a male soldier who engaged in consensual oral sodomy with a female civilian in a military barracks. Although the case involved heterosexual conduct, it appears to be the first decision by a military tribunal to recognize a right to engage in consensual adult sodomy, under principles that may be equally applicable to Article 125 prosecutions targeting homosexual activity.[65]

Meanwhile, only two federal courts of appeals have issued decisions in cases involving post- *Lawrence* challenges to "don't ask, don't tell," and both of these courts have grappled with questions regarding the standard of review that should apply. The problem is that the *Lawrence* decision did not explicitly deem the right to engage in private consensual homosexual conduct to be a "fundamental" liberty interest, nor did the Court specifically identify the standard of review to be used in the future. Indeed, the decision appeared to apply neither traditional rational basis review nor strict scrutiny.

Identifying the standard of judicial review to apply was the central issue in *Witt v. Department of the Air Force*,[66] a recent decision in which the Court of Appeals for the Ninth Circuit reinstated a lawsuit against the military's "don't ask, don't tell" policy. In 2004, Major Margaret Witt, a decorated Air Force officer who had been in a long-term relationship with another woman was placed under investigation for being a homosexual. Although Witt shared a home 250 miles away from base with her partner, never engaged in homosexual acts while on base, and never disclosed her sexual orientation, the Air Force initiated formal separation proceedings against her due to her homosexuality. Witt filed suit in district court, claiming that the "don't ask, don't tell" policy violated her constitutional right to procedural due process, substantive due process, and equal protection, but the district court dismissed her suit for failure to state a claim.[67] The Ninth Circuit affirmed the district court's dismissal of the equal protection claim, but remanded the procedural and substantive due process claims to the district court for further consideration.

Finding that the result in *Lawrence* was "inconsistent with the minimal protections afforded by traditional rational basis review" and that the cases upon which the *Lawrence* Court relied all involved heightened scrutiny, the Ninth Circuit ultimately held that "*Lawrence* applied something more than traditional rational basis review," but left open the question whether the Court had applied strict scrutiny, intermediate scrutiny, or a different type of heightened scrutiny.[68] Hesitating to apply traditional strict scrutiny to Witt's claim in the absence of the application of "narrow tailoring" and "compelling governmental interest" requirements in *Lawrence*, the Ninth Circuit instead looked to another Supreme Court case that had applied a heightened level of scrutiny to a substantive due process claim.[69] Extrapolating from its analysis of this case, the Ninth Circuit concluded:

> We hold that when the government attempts to intrude upon the personal and private lives of homosexuals, in a manner that implicates the rights identified in *Lawrence*, the government must advance an important governmental interest, the intrusion must significantly further that interest, and the intrusion must be necessary to further that interest. In other words, for the third factor, a less intrusive means must be unlikely to achieve substantially the government's interest.... In addition, we hold that this heightened scrutiny analysis is as- applied rather than facial.... Under this

> review, we must determine not whether ['don't ask, don't tell'] has some hypothetical, post hoc rationalization in general, but whether a justification exists for the application of the policy as applied to Major Witt.[70]

Although the court ruled that the government clearly advances an important governmental interest in management of the military, the court was unable to determine from the existing record whether "don't ask, don't tell" satisfies the second and third factors and therefore remanded the case to district court for further development of the record. It is important to note that even if the district court does ultimately find in favor of Major Witt, the decision would not invalidate the "don't ask, don't tell" policy. Unlike a facial claim, in which the constitutionality of a statute is evaluated on it face as if it applies to all hypothetical plaintiffs, the Ninth Circuit directed that the constitutional inquiry in *Witt* be conducted on an "as applied" basis. As a result, the impact of any decision by the district court would be limited to Major Witt and would not apply to other plaintiffs, who would be required to file their own individual claims.

Shortly after the Ninth Circuit issued its opinion in the *Witt* case, the Court of Appeals for the First Circuit handed down a decision upholding a lower court's dismissal of a challenge to "don't ask, don't tell" brought by 12 gay and lesbian veterans who had been discharged under the policy. In the case, *Cook v. Gates*,[71] the First Circuit agreed with much of the Ninth Circuit's reasoning in *Witt*, although the opinions differed in some important respects. Like the Ninth Circuit, the First Circuit concluded that the *Lawrence* case "did indeed recognize a protected liberty interest for adults to engage in private, consensual sexual intimacy and applied a balancing of constitutional interests that defies either the strict scrutiny or rational basis label."[72] In contrast to the Ninth Circuit, however, the First Circuit evaluated the claim as a facial challenge and concluded that the plaintiffs' challenge failed. According to the court, the *Lawrence* decision recognized only a narrowly defined liberty interest in consensual adult sexual activity that excludes other types of sexual conduct, including homosexual conduct by service members.[73] Although the First Circuit noted that an as-applied challenge might involve conduct that does fall within *Lawrence's* protected liberty interest—such as homosexual conduct occurring off-base between consenting adults—the court nevertheless concluded that such as-applied challenges fail when balanced against the governmental interest in preserving military effectiveness.[74] As a result, the court dismissed the plaintiffs' as-applied challenge.

In summary, historically undergirding the judicial approach to military policies regarding homosexuals has been a tradition of deference to Congress and the Executive in the regulation of military affairs. The *Lawrence* decision marked out a constitutional safe harbor for private homosexual conduct between consenting adults in the civilian sphere founded on due process principles. Cases pending now and in the future may call on the courts to reconcile these precedents in evaluating the constitutionality of "don't ask, don't tell" and Article 125.

Actions Following the Murder of Private Barry Winchell

Following the murder of Army Private First Class (Pfc.) Barry Winchell in 1999 at Fort Campbell, KY, efforts were made by numerous groups to change or create new policies due to allegations of homosexual harassment on military bases.

The killing of Pfc. Winchell had implications beyond the specifics of his case, including judicial, legislative, and administrative actions. Some of these involved administrative and legislative actions concerning hate crimes. Others involved legislative and administrative actions involving those in the chain of command, including the reassignment of individuals and senatorial holds being placed on the consideration of certain promotions. This case generated a large amount of media and political attention.[75]

Winchell's death was connected in part to his off-duty romantic relationship with a biologically male pre-operative transsexual. This relationship became intertwined with a relationship Winchell had with another soldier, his roommate, Specialist Justin Fisher. The complications of these relationships led to a fight between Winchell and a third soldier during a barracks party. Winchell, it is reported, had the upper hand in the fight. On July 6, 1999, Private Calvin Glover, who had lost the fight, entered the hallway where Winchell was sleeping and bludgeoned him to death with a baseball bat. Fisher, soon after, entered the hallway and reportedly tried to assist Glover in cleaning up the scene. Both Glover and Fisher were arrested.[76] Press reports of the incident labeled it a 'hate crime.'[77] Glover was tried by court-martial and received a life sentence. Fisher was sentenced to 12 and 1/2 years imprisonment as part of a plea bargain.[78]

Winchell's murder became an example and focal point for gay-rights groups and some in the media who criticized military leaders at Fort Campbell over the incident.[79] Some suggested that the "don't ask, don't tell" policy was responsible for Winchell's death. They claimed that "don't ask, don't tell" reinforces negative attitudes toward homosexuals in uniform, because the policy treats homosexuals differently than heterosexuals in uniform. As such, it is claimed that this policy fostered an atmosphere of "homophobia" in the military that encouraged violence against homosexuals. Others contend that Winchell's death occurred in spite of the policy and that the incidents in question would not have occurred had he and Fisher abided by its provisions. Under this policy, homosexual behavior does not become an issue for those in uniform because it must be kept "personal and private." These individuals cite the death of Winchell and the incarceration of Fisher and Glover as classic examples of how open homosexuality in the ranks can lead to "disruptions to good order and discipline" that "don't ask, don't tell" was designed to prevent.

Many in the media and homosexual rights advocacy groups viewed the Winchell murder as representative of homophobia in the services or, at the least, lax attitudes toward preventing the harassment of those suspected of being homosexual. Partly in response to Winchell's murder, in October 1999, President Clinton signed an executive order modifying the Uniform Code of Military Justice (UCMJ) by allowing evidence to be presented during the sentencing phase of a trial that a violent crime can be considered a hate crime.[80]

In response to concerns over the handling of the case, both the Army and DOD Inspectors General (IG) investigated the incident. Later, the DOD IG released a report on March 24, 2000. "The [DOD] IG found the command climate at Winchell's post, Fort Campbell, Ky., was generally supportive and healthy. But the report said Winchell's company in the 101st Airborne Division (Air Assault) was marred by poor morale because of an abusive first sergeant who has since been replaced.... The Defense Department IG, in March, found that anti-gay attitudes were 'commonplace' and widely tolerated in the military. When the report was released, Defense Secretary William Cohen launched a task force headed by Air Force Under Secretary Carol DiBattiste, to develop a plan to reduce harassment of all kinds within the ranks."[81]

On July 21, 2000, little more than a year after Winchell's murder, Under Secretary of Defense (Personnel and Readiness), Bernard Rostker, announced the introduction of a DOD Anti-Harassment Action Plan (AHAP) adopting the principle of "treating all individuals with dignity and respect" and noting that "mistreatment, harassment, [including that based on sexual orientation], and inappropriate comments or gestures," have no place in the armed forces.[82] Then-Secretary of Defense, William Cohen, approved the plan and forwarded it to the Services for implementation.[83] The AHAP is a 13 point plan recommending anti-harassment training, reporting of harassment, enforcement against harassment, and measurement to assess adherence to anti-harassment policies as well as the effectiveness of such policies.

Following a report in May, 2003, by the Servicemembers Legal Defense Network (SLDN) claiming that the military had failed to issue a directive regarding AHAP, several Members of Congress wrote a letter to Secretary of Defense Rumsfeld asking DOD to implement the AHAP. Although the AHAP has been implemented, it appears that SLDN's focus is on the lack of an overarching DOD Directive. In a recent report, SLDN states:

> The Bush Administration and its Pentagon leaders continue to ignore a growing epidemic of anti-gay harassment within the armed forces.... Despite the adoption of a comprehensive Anti-Harassment Action Plan ... Defense Department leaders refuse to implement the plan and continue to turn a blind eye to dangerous harassment within the ranks.... [T]he plan continues to collect dust on Pentagon shelves.[84]

In response, the Under Secretary of Defense (Personnel and Readiness), David Chu, in a June 24, 2004 letter to Congress, described existing Service policies and programs as "sufficient to address" harassment.[85]

> The Department has determined the over-arching directive recommended by the Plan is not necessary. The Services' policies and programs are sufficient to address this important issue. It is the Department's view that all service members should be treated with dignity and respect. This is a value held by all four Services and a cornerstone of our leadership and human resource strategies that is reflected in the core values and institutional training throughout the Department.[86]

In this letter, Under Secretary Chu describes anti-harassment efforts implemented by the Services, including training, reporting, measurement and enforcement.

Independent of these actions, Winchell's parents filed a $1.8 million wrongful death claim against the military and were twice rebuffed. [87]

Critics continued their focus on the military leadership at Fort Campbell. The Army IG investigation found nothing to implicate the Commanding General of the 101st Airborne Division at Fort Campbell, Maj. Gen. Robert T. Clark, who convened the court-martial of Fisher and Glover. Later, when the Army decided to transfer Clark (for reasons unrelated to the Winchell murder) to become vice director of operations for the Joint Chiefs of Staff (JCS) at the

Pentagon, gay rights advocates and several Members of Congress objected, with 30 Members of the House writing to then-Secretary of Defense William Cohen "urging that he hold the general responsible for what appears to have been a highly charged environment at Fort Campbell in the months before Private Winchell's death."[88] In October 2002, when Clark was nominated for promotion to Lieutenant General as Commander of the Fifth U.S. Army, Winchell's parents, gay rights groups, and People for the American Way, asked the Senate to block his nomination.[89] A hold was placed on the 2002 nomination of Clark to prevent a floor vote. Over a year later, the Senate approved the nomination.[90] In November, 2003, Clark became the Commanding General, Fifth United States Army, Fort Sam Houston, TX. Lieutenant General Robert T. Clark retired on February 1, 2007.

During this period, efforts to include hate crime legislation in both the FY2001 and FY2005 National Defense Authorization Acts failed.[91] In both years, the Senate bills included language that would permit the Attorney General to provide assistance at the request of state, local, and Indian tribe officials in the investigation and prosecution of hate crimes. This language also included a provision that would allow the Attorney General to award grants to state, local, and Indian tribe law enforcement officials to assist with the investigation and prosecution of such crimes. The language would also amend chapter 13 of title 18 United States Code to "establish a substantive federal prohibition of certain specific hate crime acts." However, in both instances, the House bill contained no similar provision and the Senate receded, thereby dropping the provisions in conference.

H.R. 1585, the National Defense Authorization Act for Fiscal Year 2008, was passed by both the House and the Senate. It contained language concerning hate crimes that would involve substantial changes in Title 18, United States Code. These changes were not necessarily specific to the military. Objecting to this and other provisions in H.R. 1585, the President vetoed the bill on December 28, 2007. Much of the language in this bill (excluding the provisions on hate crimes) was reintroduced as H.R. 4986, and was passed by Congress and signed by the President, becoming P.L. 110-118 on January 29, 2008.

Recruiting, JROTC, ROTC and Campus Policies

Congressional concerns over military access to campuses for recruiting purposes have led to the enactment of legislative proposals over the years.

Colloquially known as the "Solomon amendments"[92] or "Solomon-Pombo amendments," [P.L. 103-337; 108 Stat. 2776; October 5, 1994] in recognition of its earlier proponents, this language sought to afford military recruiters and Reserve Officer Training Corps access to campuses and students.

Many colleges, universities, and in some cases, high school campuses, have been in the vanguard of the effort to expand civil rights for homosexuals. In certain cases, schools have sought to challenge DOD policy pertaining to homosexuals including taking steps to limit or eliminate various types of military presence on campus. For example, in certain instances, military personnel have been prevented from recruiting on campus, and actions have been taken to limit or sever Reserve Officer Training Corps (ROTC) connections with the campus.

Generally speaking, efforts to recruit on high school and college campuses have been addressed separately in legislation. For purposes of clarity, they are also treated separately here.

High Schools

In 1982, as part of long-standing recruiting concerns, Congress passed language *allowing* the Secretary of Defense to "collect and compile directory information pertaining to each student who is 17 years of age or older or in eleventh grade ... or higher and who is enrolled in a secondary school in the United States or its territories, possessions, or in the Commonwealth of Puerto Rico."[93] The collection of this information was limited to three years for any individual, and further limited to name, address, telephone listing, date and place of birth, level of education, degrees received, and most recent educational agency or institution attended, and was required to be kept confidential. Nothing in the law required or authorized the Secretary to *require* any educational institution to furnish the information.[94] The collection of this information, or further, the matter of recruiter access to the campuses, however voluntary, were not without some controversy.[95]

For example, in 1998, two high schools broke with the Portland (OR) School Board by allowing military recruiters on campus.[96] Proponents of the ban insisted they were opposing discrimination against homosexuals by the military. Critics contend the school board was merely, and "hypocritically" substituting discrimination against the military in favor of a homosexual rights agenda.[97]

In recent years, the congressional legislative activity concerning the recruiting of high school students has increased. In 1999, Congress enacted language *requesting* secondary schools to provide DOD with the "same access to secondary school students, and to directory information concerning such students, as is provided generally to post-secondary educational institutions or to prospective employers of those students."[98] Despite this change—previously, DOD had been *allowed* to compile such information—recruiter access to secondary schools in some cases continued to meet resistance.[99]

The following year (2000), Congress enacted language stating that the educational agencies concerned *shall* provide such recruiter access to campus and to directory information. If a request for this access were denied, this language instructed the services to send an appropriate designated officer or official to meet with the agency. If, after a meeting, such access continued to be denied, the services were to notify the designated state official (such as a Governor) and request access. Should the denial of access continue, the Secretary of Defense was instructed to notify the Secretary of Education. Upon determination by the Secretary of Defense that the denial is extended to at least two of the military services (including the Coast Guard), congressional committees, and the respective Senators and Representatives of the jurisdictions involved were to be notified. Certain schools could be excluded from this process: specifically, private schools that maintained a religious objection to service in the armed forces; or, in the case of a local educational agency, a policy resulting from majority vote of denying such access.[100]

In 2001, Congress strengthened this language by *requiring* local educational agencies who are receiving assistance under the Elementary and Secondary Educational Act to provide recruiters with the access to students and directories that had been *requested* in 1999. In addition, the language provided that students with parental consent, or the parent alone on behalf of the student, could opt out of having the student's information released. [101]

In 2002, the "No Child Left Behind Act" stated that as a condition of receiving funds under the act, local educational institutions were required, upon request, to provide recruiter access to directory information. Opt-out provisions were included as before, as were exceptions for private schools with religious objections to military service.[102]

It has been reported that certain educational agencies and others have taken an active role in limiting such access. Primarily, this is done by sending 'opt-out' forms to students and/or parents.[103] Many educational agencies and secondary schools, however, *have* provided recruiter access and access to directory information. Also, hundreds of thousands of secondary students participate in federally funded Junior Reserve Officers Training Corps at affiliated secondary schools. [104]

Finally, in 2003, Congress amended the law by removing the provision that had allowed for a majority vote of the local educational agency to deny recruiter access or access to directory information thereby removing one impediment to such access.[105]

In 2007, DOD announced changes concerning how it treats information in its military recruiting database following a settlement with the New York Civil Liberties Union. DOD agreed to use the database only for recruiting and not to share that data with other government agencies. DOD agreed to destroy information on individuals after three rather than five years. DOD also agreed to collect social security numbers only from the Selective Service System.[106]

Although some school districts have attempted to eliminate military recruiting on their campuses, such efforts have generally been short-lived. For example, the San Francisco Board of Education recently abandoned its effort to eliminate Junior ROTC from its schools, and a federal court recently struck down several laws that would have prohibited military recruiters from contacting minors in two California cities.[107]

Colleges and Universities

Even prior to the 1993 "don't ask, don't tell" compromise, the exclusion of homosexuals from military service, and hence, ROTC, had proven to be problematic on some college campuses.[108] (From 1986 to 1994, 28 students reportedly were discharged from ROTC on grounds of homosexuality and nine were ordered to repay their scholarships.) In May 1990, for example, it was reported that two students from Harvard and the Massachusetts Institute of Technology were dismissed from the Navy ROTC program at MIT. The Navy sought recoupment of its scholarship funds (totaling over $80,000 for both students). The provost of MIT, John Deutch, wrote to then- Secretary of Defense Richard Cheney, stating that it was "wrong and shortsighted" to maintain "the ROTC policy not to accept gay or lesbian students into its programs and to require avowed homosexuals to disenroll and pay back their scholarship funds." After reviewing the cases on the merits, the Navy made a decision not to seek recoupment from these two students.[109]

On May 17, 1994, then-Deputy Defense Secretary John Deutch issued a directive. Under that directive, and based on the "don't ask, don't tell" compromise, Service secretaries could seek recoupment of ROTC scholarships when there were violations of military law; however, the Service secretaries would not seek recoupment for homosexuality. Individuals using a claim of homosexuality as a means of avoiding military service were likely to be required to repay their scholarships.[110]

Over the past 10 years, there has been considerable congressional and judicial activity on military access to colleges and universities. The National Defense Authorization Act for FY1995[111] limited efforts to interfere with military access to colleges and universities:

> No funds available to the Department of Defense may be provided by grant or contract to any institution of higher education that has a policy of denying, or which effectively prevents, the Secretary of Defense from obtaining for military recruiting purposes - (A) entry to campuses or access to students on campuses; or (B) access to directory information pertaining to students.

The above law (also know as the Solomon Amendment) further instructed the Secretary of Defense to consult with the Secretary of Education in prescribing regulations to determine when an educational institution denies or prevents access.

In 1996, Congress enacted additional language pertaining to ROTC at colleges and universities. The National Defense Authorization Act for FY1996[112] stated:

> No funds appropriated or otherwise available to the Department of Defense may be made obligated by contract or by grant (including a grant of funds to be available for student aid) to any institution of higher education that, as determined by the Secretary of Defense, has an anti-ROTC policy and at which, as determined by the Secretary, the Secretary would otherwise maintain or seek to establish a unit of the Senior Reserve Officer Training Corps or at which the Secretary would otherwise enroll or seek to enroll students for participation in a unit of the Senior Reserve Officer Training Corps at another nearby institution of higher education.

This law required the Secretary to notify the Secretary of Education, Senate Armed Services Committee and the then-House National Security Committee (now House Armed Services Committee) when such a determination had been made. In addition, every six months the Secretary was required to publish a list of ineligible institutions in the Federal Register.

The Connecticut Supreme Court, in 1996, upheld a lower court ruling that the DOD policy on homosexuality violated the state's 1991 Gay Rights Law barring discrimination on the basis of "sexual orientation" and, therefore, military recruiters could be permanently banned from the University of Connecticut Law School campus in Hartford.[113] These actions led to a seemingly contradictory situation. Although military recruiters were barred from the law school campus, the University of Connecticut maintained military ROTC units on its Storrs campus. The University of Connecticut (UConn) has been designated, by the state legislature, a land-grant university. Under the Morrill Act,[114] as signed by President Lincoln in 1862, institutions aided under the act must teach military tactics along with their regular curriculum. ROTC fulfills this requirement.[115] Thus, due to the court ruling, military recruiters were prohibited from recruiting at the UConn law school in Hartford, but the university maintains an ROTC unit at its campus in Storrs. This campus continued to enroll students in ROTC and accepted federal funding. The presence of, and continued enrollment by, this ROTC unit may also have been in conflict with the state's 1991 Gay Rights Law prohibiting discrimination on the basis of "sexual orientation."

The Omnibus Appropriations Act for FY1997[116] contained language that limited the ability of educational institutions, or sub-elements thereof (such as a law school or a satellite campus), to block ROTC programs or recruiter access. Under this language, funds made available in this or other relevant appropriations, including contracts or grants (such as student aid), would not be available to any covered institution that denied or prevented access by military recruiters or prevented the maintaining, establishing or the operation of an ROTC program. Three exceptions were written into the law [110 Stat. 3009-270]: (1) "the covered educational entity has ceased the policy or practice [of discriminating against the military]; (2) the institution of higher education has a longstanding policy of pacifism based on historical religious affiliation; or (3) the institution of higher education involved is prohibited by the law of any State, or by the order of any State court, from allowing Senior Reserve Officer Training Corps activities or Federal recruiting on campus, except that this paragraph shall apply only during the one-year period beginning on the effective date.... " In the summer of 1997, DOD published a list of offending schools in the Federal Register. Of the 27 schools on the list, 17 were in Connecticut. By August 22, 1997, the list was reduced to 22 schools, 17 from Connecticut.

In a seemingly ironic twist, service members who receive tuition assistance from the military would see this assistance terminated if they attended one of the schools listed. In order to address this situation, language was included in the FY1998 National Defense Authorization Act conference report:

> The conferees are aware that the Connecticut State Legislature and the State Supreme Court have taken steps to prohibit military recruiting on the campuses of state funded colleges and universities. As a result of this prohibition, ... the Department of Defense suspended payment of contract and grant funding to these colleges and universities.
>
> The conferees note that the Connecticut State Legislature is not scheduled to meet until February 1998. The Governor has pledged that he will ensure the passage of legislation that would remedy the matter concerning access of military recruiters to Connecticut state institutions of higher education.
>
> In order to provide the State of Connecticut with the opportunity to repeal its prohibition, the conferees direct the Secretary of Defense not to use funds that would have been used for contracts or grants to higher education institutions in Connecticut as sources in a reprogramming request nor to submit such funds as part of a rescission offer until March 29, 1998. If the State of Connecticut has not repealed the prohibition as of March 29, 1998, the Secretary of Defense may use the funds in a reprogramming or rescission activity.
>
> Notwithstanding this sequestering of funds, the conferees insist that military recruiters be afforded access to institutions of higher education or face the consequence of loss of federal funds.[117]

In response, on October 29, 1997, the Governor called a one-day special session of the state legislature to consider the matter. "[B]oth houses of the General Assembly approved the change [allowing the military to recruit on state campuses] by overwhelming margins. The Governor signed the bill the next day."[118]

In 1999, Congress modified the law yet again. Under this modification, federal funds in the form of student financial assistance could not be withheld from students attending schools that violated the law with regard to recruiter access and ROTC.[119]

Opposition to these varied restrictions took a number of forms. Many law schools, in particular, sought ways to mollify, "ameliorate," or terminate these restrictions. For example, it was reported that law professors Carol Chomsky and Margaret Montoya, co-presidents of the Society of American Law Teachers (SALT), sent a letter to associate deans listing 27 "action items" in response to the "threat" of military recruiting. Among items cited:

> Designate a particular person in the Dean's or Associate Dean's office to ... make sure on an ongoing basis, that law school resources, including career

services, are not used to facilitate any on-campus recruiting by the military....[120]

While some have viewed these efforts as intended to harass recruiters, others point out that these efforts and others are merely supporting campus non-discrimination policies.

On February 2, 2005, the House of Representatives voted in favor of H.Con.Res. 36 (327-84):

> *Resolved by the House of Representatives (the Senate concurring),* That—
>
> (1) Congress remains committed to the achievement of military personnel readiness through vigorous application of the requirements set forth in section 983 of title 10, United States Code, relating to equal access for military recruiters at installations of higher education, and will explore all options necessary to maintain this commitment, including the powers vested under article I, section 9, of the Constitution;[121]
>
> (2) it is the sense of Congress that the executive branch should aggressively continue to pursue measures to challenge any decision impeding or prohibiting the operation of section 983 of title 10, United States Code; and
>
> (3) Congress encourages the executive branch to follow the doctrine of non-acquiescence and not find a decision affecting one jurisdiction to be binding on other jurisdictions.[122]

Supreme Court Review of the Solomon Amendment

Under the Solomon Amendment, as noted, specified federal funds may not be provided to an "institution of higher education," or "subelement" of such an institution, if the institution or subelement "has a policy or practice" that "either prohibits, or in effect prevents" military recruiters from gaining access to campuses or students "in a manner that is at least equal in quality and scope to the access to campuses and to students that is provided to any other employer."[123] The Solomon Amendment applies to all institutions of higher education except ones with "a longstanding policy of pacifism based on historical religious affiliation."[124] The act governs all funds made available through the DOD, the Department of Homeland Security, the Department of Health and Human Services, the Central Intelligence Agency, and other enumerated agencies.[125] It does not apply to funds provided to educational institutions or individuals "solely for student financial assistance, related administrative costs, or costs associated with attendance."[126]

In *Rumsfeld v. Forum for Academic and Institutional Rights (FAIR),*[127] the Supreme Court unanimously rejected arguments by the Forum for Academic and Individual Rights, an association of law schools and professors, that it was unconstitutional for the federal government to condition university funding on compliance with the Solomon Amendment. Previously, a divided Third Circuit panel had agreed that the Solomon Amendment had compelled the law schools to convey messages of support for the military's policy of discriminatory exclusion, but the Court reversed the lower court's decision. The appellate panel had relied in part on a 2000 Supreme Court decision, *Dale v. Boy Scouts of America* [128]—which held that the Boy Scouts have an expressive right to exclude gay scoutmasters—for the converse proposition that the nation's universities have a right to "expressive association" in opposing military recruiters where there is a conflict between the DOD stance on sexual orientation and academic nondiscrimination policies.

In the case, the universities objected that because of the military's "don't ask, don't tell" policy, permitting recruiters on campus would undermine their policies against discrimination and that the federal law therefore violated their free speech rights. FAIR's core argument was that the Solomon Amendment amounts to an "unconstitutional condition" because it exacts a penalty for the law schools' engaging in First Amendment expressive conduct. While the government may impose reasonable conditions on the receipt of federal largesse, respondents contended, it "cannot attach strings to a benefit to 'produce a result which [it] could not command directly.'"[129] When a law school violates the equal access rule, the government threatens loss of funding not only to the law school but to the entire university. Thus, they claimed, requiring equal access forces laws schools to "propagate, accommodate, [or] subsidize an unwanted message."[130]

The government countered by pointing to the plenary powers of Congress to "raise and support armies" and to "provide for the common Defence."[131] The Third Circuit decision could "undermine military recruitment in a time of war," it argued, while neither the law schools' right to free speech nor to expressive association were infringed by allowing military recruiters to conduct on campus interviews.[132] In particular, the Solicitor General distinguished the *Boy Scouts* case in that "recruiters are not a part of the institution itself and do not become members through their recruiting activities."[133] Recruiters speak for their employers, the brief claims, not the schools, unlike the scoutmaster who represented the Boy Scouts in the earlier case. Moreover, the government emphasized that the law schools remain free to protest the military's message as long as they give recruiters equal access. If the schools choose not to allow equal access, it was argued, they simply forego funding.

In general, the Court was receptive to each of the government's arguments. First, the Court was unmoved by FAIR's theory of unconstitutional conditions, largely because of fatal flaws they found in the law schools' First Amendment analysis. This unsettled area of the law, however, may be further obscured by the observation that indirect compulsion by Congress via "a funding condition cannot be unconstitutional if it could be constitutionally imposed directly." Whether this implies that Congress may even legislate access for military recruiters (to college campuses and elsewhere), regardless of federal funding or federal policy with respect to all other recruiters, may be a fertile subject for future legal debates.

On the question of whether the Solomon Amendment impairs the First Amendment rights of the objecting institutions, the Court's opinion rejected all three arguments put forward by the law schools. First, while expressive conduct may be subject to First Amendment scrutiny,

> there is nothing in this case approaching a Government-mandated pledge or motto that the school must endorse ... [and] ... 'it has never been deemed an abridgement of speech or press to make a course of conduct illegal merely because the conduct was in part initiated, evidenced, or carried out by means of language.'[134]

Otherwise, practices having nothing to do with government dictating the content of speech— expressing disapproval of the Internal Revenue Service by refusing to pay taxes, for example— would enjoy First Amendment protection. Requiring law schools to facilitate recruiters' access by sending out e-mails and scheduling military visits were deemed "a far cry from the compelled speech" found in earlier cases. "Accommodating the military's message does not affect the law school's speech, because the schools are not speaking when they host interviews and recruiting receptions."[135] Nor, the opinion finds, would they be endorsing, or be seen as endorsing, the military policies to which they object. "A law school's decision to allow recruiters on campus is not inherently expressive."[136]

Secondly, the Court distinguished the doctrine of "expressive association," as applied by *Dale v. Boy Scouts of America.*[137] "If the government were free to restrict individuals' ability to join together and speak, it could essentially silence views that the First Amendment is intended to protect." Such was not the situation here, however, according to the Court. Merely allowing recruiters on campus and providing them with the same services as other recruiters did not require the schools to "associate" with them. Nor did it prevent their expressing opposition to military policies in other ways. They could put up signs, they could picket, they could make speeches, and they could hold forums of protest. Moreover, unlike the *Boy Scouts* case, no group membership practices or affiliations were implicated by the Solomon Amendment. Recruiters do not become components of the law schools—like the Scout leaders there—but "are, by definition, outsiders who come onto campus for [a] limited purpose" and "not to become members of the school's expressive association."[138]

Finally, the Court recognized as "[beyond] dispute" that Congress has "broad and sweeping" powers over military manpower and personnel matters—"includ[ing]the authority to require campus access for military recruiters"—the exercise of which is generally entitled to judicial "deference." Accordingly, in rejecting FAIR's position, the Court concluded:

> The issue is not whether other means of raising an army and providing for a Navy might be adequate ... (regulations are not 'invalid' simply because there is some other imaginable alternative that might be less burdensome on speech). That is a judgment for Congress, not the courts ... It suffices that the means chosen by Congress add to the effectiveness of military recruitment.[139]

Homosexuals and Marriages

Under current law, marriages are covered under the domestic relations laws of the various states. Only a handful of states currently allow same sex marriages.[140] However, Title 10, U.S.C. sec. 654(b)(3) requires the separation of service members who have married or attempted to marry a same-sex partner. Some have speculated that legal challenges to this prohibition on same-sex marriage should be anticipated. Others wonder about the ultimate resolution of a case in which individuals who have served and retired from the services then marry a same-sex partner, and then make claims for service-related benefits, such as benefits under the Survivor Benefits Plan. Currently, the Defense of Marriage Act[141] prohibits extending federal benefits to same-sex partners, and the Supreme Court has not ruled on the constitutionality of this law. What effect the changing legal landscape regarding same-sex marriage will have on military service or benefits is not clear at this time. According to DOD, it has not encountered a situation in which a retiree married to a same-sex partner has sought benefits for his or her partner.

Foreign Military Experiences

A number of foreign militaries, notably those of Great Britain, have voluntarily changed or been ordered (by court decree, for example) to change their policies with regard to homosexuals. In the case of Great Britain, the ban on homosexuals serving was lifted in January 2000, following a European Court of Human Rights ruling that the ban was unlawful. The press has reported that "A confidential Ministry of Defense review states that the introduction of gays has had no adverse effects on the operational effectiveness of the forces."[142] Australia voluntarily lifted its ban by government decree in November 1992 seemingly without problems.[143] Conversely, in July 2003, Russia lifted its ban, but the head of the Defense Ministry's health commission, Major General Valery Kulikov said, "I would not advise such persons to publicize their sexual orientation. In the army they are not liked and will probably be beaten."[144]

Foreign military experiences were given substantial consideration by the U.S. Senate in its 1993 hearings on homosexuality and the military. Although information concerning these military experiences may prove useful to U.S. policy makers, their relevance is not entirely clear. During the hearings, Prof. Charles Moskos stated:

> Comparative analysis can shed light on some of the policy issues with regards to gays and straights in the armed forces. Due attention must be paid to both points of difference and similarity. For sure, certain lessons can be drawn from the experience with gays in the militaries of other countries. But inasmuch as the United States has the most formidable military force in the world, it could also be argued that such countries might draw lessons from the United States.[145]

Indeed, there are problems in considering foreign military comparisons. For example, international variations in the definition of "homosexual" or "orientation" make comparisons difficult. Additionally, military recruiting structures (e.g., draft versus volunteers), force structures (certain foreign armed forces personnel are represented by unions), roles and missions (home guard, para-military forces, or forces subject to international deployment) suggest limits on the relevance of any such foreign comparison to actually making policy. As noted in the hearings, many countries maintain a distinction between the stated policies and the policy in practice. In addition, as noted during the hearings, "A look at official [foreign] regulations and statements rarely captures the realties of how persons of different sexual orientations are treated in their respective militaries." Furthermore, certain countries allow homosexuals to serve but do so in a manner that would arguably not be legally allowed in the United States. For example, some countries allow open homosexuals to serve, but they can "opt out" of such service if they choose (e.g., Netherlands). Other countries allow homosexuals to serve, but their promotion opportunities may be limited (e.g., Germany). Some countries have religious and/or other principles that prevent openly homosexual individuals from serving (e.g., Saudi Arabia, Iran).

End Notes

[1] "[H]e elicited approving whoops when he said he would sign an executive order to eliminate discrimination based on sexual orientation in the US military." Wilkie, Curtis, Harvard tosses warmup queries to Clinton on eve of N.H. debate, *Boston Globe*, October 31, 1991: 22.

[2] President's News Conference, in *Public Papers of the Presidents of the United States, William J. Clinton, 1993, Book 1*, January 29, 1993: published 1994: 20.

[3] See *Congressional Record*, February 4, 1993, S2 163 -S2245.

[4] President's News Conference, in *Public Papers of the Presidents of the United States, William J. Clinton, 1993, Book 1*, July 19, 1993: published 1994: 1111.

[5] According to a Senior Administration official, ... [W]e think that probably the most significant advance is heightened—no witch hunts, no pursuit policy. So I think it's fair to call this policy 'don't ask, don't tell, don't pursue.'" White House Briefing, Federal News Service, July 16, 1993.

[6] "The previous policy was, ask, do not tell, investigate. The [proposed] policy is, do not ask, do not tell, do not investigate." Secretary of Defense, Les Aspin, U.S. Congress. Senate. Committee on Armed Services, Hearings, Policy Concerning Homosexuality in the Armed Forces, Senate Hearings 103-845, 103rd Cong., 2nd Sess., 1994: 746. "And even Secretary of Defense Les Aspin seemed a bit confused about the Clinton administration's new policy allowing homosexuals in the military, expressing doubt as to whether a single acknowledgment of homosexuality by a service member would constitute grounds for discharge... But grasping [the policy's] details could prove difficult, as Aspin himself demonstrated yesterday in response to a question from Sen. Jeff Bingaman (D-N.M.). The senator asked Aspin what would happen in the case of a homosexual soldier who reveals his sexual orientation to another soldier, who then reports the conversation to a commander. At first, Aspin said flatly that such a disclosure would not be grounds for dismissal.... But that brought a puzzled response from [committee chairman, Sen.] Nunn, who quoted Aspin as saying in his opening remarks that homosexual 'statements' were a form of prohibited

conduct.... At that point, Aspin seemed to shift position." Lancaster, John, "Senators Find Clinton Policy on Gays in the Military Confusing," *Washington Post*, July 21, 1993: A12.

[7] An administrative discharge is designated as 'Honorable,' 'General,' or 'Other than Honorable,' and is provided by an executive decision reflecting the nature of the service performed by the member. A 'Bad Conduct' or 'Dishonorable' discharge can only be awarded via a court-martial during sentencing. As discussed in the section entitled "Discharge Statistics," the vast majority of homosexuals who are discharged receive administrative discharges and most of those are designated 'Honorable.'

See the hearings with then-Secretary of Defense Aspin and others following release of the July 19, 1993 Memorandum, U.S. Congress. Senate. Committee on Armed Services, Hearings, Policy Concerning Homosexuality in the Armed Forces, Senate Hearings 103-845, 103rd Cong., 2nd Sess., 1994: 700 et seq.

[8] " ... [T]he complex nature of the compromise was evident in the puzzlement of committee members who described [the policy] as confusing, contradictory and an invitation to endless litigation in the courts." Lancaster, July 21, 1993. "Clinton interpreted this language at a news conference yesterday to mean that gay service personnel do 'not necessarily' have to remain in the closet. The senior Pentagon official acknowledged, however, that homosexuals probably will not be able to disclose their sexual orientation.", Lancaster, John, "Policy Tosses Issue to Courts, Ambiguity Seen Leading to Protracted Litigation," *Washington Post*, July 20, 1993: A1.

[9] "Clinton was also asked by a reporter whether he would direct his Justice Department, which had days before been in ... [court] arguing for the ban, not to appeal the anti-ban ruling, but he did not answer.... Today, the Clinton Department of Justice has not only appealed the anti-ban ruling but is arguing in court that the government can discriminate on the basis of sexual orientation." Burr, Chandler, reprinted from *California Lawyer Magazine*, June, 1994.

[10] Secretary of Defense, Les Aspin stated, "The Chiefs understood that the Commander-in-Chief wanted to change the existing policy to end discrimination based solely on status. The President understood that it was extremely important that any changes occur in a way that maintained the high level of morale and unit cohesion which is so important for military readiness and effectiveness." Secretary of Defense, Les Aspin, (with DOD General Counsel, Jamie Gorelick), News Conference, Reuter Transcript Report, December 23, 1993: 1.

[11] U.S. Department of Defense, Secretary of Defense, *Memorandum for the Secretaries of the Army, Navy, Air Force, and Chairman of the Joint Chiefs of Staff*, July 19, 1993.

[12] Office of the Assistant Secretary of Defense, (Public Affairs), News Release, December 22, 1993.

[13] U.S. Department of Defense, Office of the Assistant Secretary of Defense (Public Affairs), News Release, No. 605- 93, *Directives Implementing the New DOD Policy on Homosexual Conduct in the Armed Forces*, December 22, 1993.

[14] U.S. Department of Defense, Office of the Assistant Secretary of Defense (P&R), *Qualification Standards for Enlistment, Appointment and Induction*, Directive1304.26, December 21, 1993, incorporating change 1, March 4, 1994: 9.

[15] U.S. Department of Defense, Assistant Secretary of Defense (P&R), Directive, *Enlisted Administrative Separations*, No. 1332.14, December 21, 1993, Incorporation Change March 4, 1994: 9. See Scarborough, Rowen, "White House cuts Phrase restricting gay discharges," *Washington Times*, February 10, 1994: A1, and, "Defense Policy on Gays Takes Effect," *Washington Post*, March 2, 1994.

[16] "Today's preferred terms and the term 'sexual orientation' itself have a variety of definitions in the literature but these generally comprise one or both of two components: a 'psychological' component and a 'behavioral' component. Not all definitions include both components, ..., definitions that include both of these components use either the conjunction 'and' or 'or' to

join them." Sell, Randall L., "Defining and Measuring Sexual Orientation: A Review," *Archives of Sexual Behavior*, Vol. 26, No. 6, 1997: 646.

[17] Scarborough, Rowen, "Pentagon memo removes winning defense for gays," *Washington Times*, December 29, 1995: A3.

[18] U.S. Department of Defense, General Counsel, Memorandum for the General Counsels of the Military Departments, Judge Advocate General of the Army, Navy, and Air Force, and the Staff Judge Advocate to the Commandant of the Marine Corps, *Policy on Homosexual Conduct in the Armed Forces*, August 18, 1995.

[19] Josh Rogan, "No Telling If "Don't Ask" Policy Will Continue," *CQ Weekly*, July 20, 2009, p. 1694.

[20] Marquis, Christopher, "Discharges of Gay Troops Rise, And So Do Bias Incidents," *New York Times*, March 14, 2002.

[21] U.S. Department of Defense, Office of the Assistant Secretary of Defense (Personnel and Readiness), Report to the Secretary of Defense, Review of the Effectiveness of the Application and Enforcement of the Department's Policy on Homosexual Conduct in the Military, April 1998: 3. This chapter stated that investigations could only be initiated after commanders receive specific and credible information concerning homosexual conduct and that inappropriate investigations occurred only in isolated instances.

[22] For example, see Moskos, Charles, "The Law Works—And Here's Why," *Army Times*, October 27, 2003: 62. "Homosexual separations for whatever reason are one-tenth of 1% of military personnel. Of those discharges, more than 80% are the result of voluntary 'statements' by service members. The number of discharges for homosexual 'acts' has declined over the past decade. Gay-rights advocates argue that the growth in discharges for statements is due largely to commanders improperly seeking out gays. Undoubtedly, that happens sometimes. Yet commanders also report being worried they might be accused of conducting 'witch hunts,' so they tend to process out an alleged homosexual only when a case of 'telling' is dumped in their laps. Let me offer another possible explanation. Whether you're gay or not, saying you are is now the quickest way out of the military with an honorable discharge. And identifying oneself as gay carries less stigma in our society than it once did. Consider that whites are proportionately three times more likely than blacks to be discharged for homosexuality. Are commanders singling out whites and investigating their sexual orientation? Highly unlikely. The stigma against homosexuality is stronger among blacks than whites, and thus blacks are less willing to declare they are gay. Gay advocates are quick to draw an analogy between the exclusion of homosexuals and racial segregation in the military. Many black soldiers find that analogy offensive." See also: Christenson, Sig, "Recruits Deny Lackland Harassment," *San Antonio Express-News*, February 7, 1999. These and other articles assert that claims of homosexuality can serve as a means of terminating a military obligation. "Mario isn't in the Army now. In March he left Fort Bragg with an honorable discharge. Some may find Mario's willingness to use his homosexuality as a means of shirking his commitment objectionable." Lamme, Robert, "Dazed in the Military," *The Advocate*, No. 673, January 24, 1995: 46.

[23] For example, see Langeland, Terje, "Gay Discharges on the Rise," INews, online at http://www.csindy.com/csindy/ 2002-05-30/news.html, May 30-June 15, 2002. "[Servicemembers Legal Defense Network] executive director, C. Dixon Osborn, said the numbers show the 'Don't Ask, Don't Tell' policy has failed... According to Dixon, the policy is being widely disregarded. 'The idea of 'Don't Ask, Don't Tell is a myth,' Osborn said. 'The Pentagon continues to ask and pursue and harass every day, which means that any of the promises that were made have gone by the wayside.'" See also, Myers, Steven Lee, "Gay Group's Study Finds Military Harassment Rising," *New York Times*, March 15, 1999. In a recent article, Sharon Alexander, an attorney for SLDN network offered the following possible explanations for the decrease in homosexual discharges, "First, there is a growing acceptance of gays serving in the military, she said, and some commanders, especially younger ones are reluctant to enforce a law they believe to be unfair.... It could be

the case, Alexander said, that with a war on, commanders in the field either don't want to lose able-bodied soldiers or they simply don't have time to worry about enforcing 'Don't Ask, Don't Tell.' ... [A Pentagon spokesman, Lt.Col. Joe] Richard dismissed those explanations as a 'fanciful analysis' by opponents of the law. There's never been a concerted effort to go on witch hunts to identify gay soldiers, he said. 'It is only when they declare themselves or openly practice their sexual preference that we have no alternative but to begin the investigative process and make a determination as to whether or not they themselves are homosexual.'" Reinert, Patty, "Is The Military Out of Step?", *Houston Chronicle*, February 6, 2005.

[24] Hull, Anne, "How 'Don't Tell' Translates," *The Washington Post*, June 18, 2004: A1.

[25] Data concerning the prevalence of homosexuality in society varies, but is reported to be approximately 1.6%. Smith, Tom W., "Adult Sexual Behavior in 1989: Number of Partners, Frequency of Intercourse and Risk of AIDS," *Family Planning Perspectives*, Vol. 23, No. 3, May/June 1991: 104. The percentage of homosexual individuals in society varies according to definitions used and sampling methods. For a broader discussion, see CRS Report 93-52, *Homosexuals and U.S. Military Personnel Policy*, by David F. Burrelli, January 14, 1993: 12 (archived report reprinted in U.S. Congress, Senate, Hearings, Policy Concerning Homosexuality in the Armed Forces, S. Hrg. 103-845, 103rd Cong., 2nd Sess., March 29, 1993: 20-94.) CRS is unaware of any reliable empirical research supporting the frequent assertion that homosexuals account for 10% of the population. See Muir, J. Gordon, "Homosexuals and the 10% Fallacy," *Wall Street Journal*, March 31, 1993.

[26] Lambert, Wade, and Stephanie Simon, "U.S. Military Moves to Discharge Some Gay Veterans of Gulf War," *Wall Street Journal*, July 30, 1991: B6.

[27] 10 U.S.C. 12305, Authority of President to suspend certain laws relating to promotion, retirement, and separation.

[28] U.S. Department of the Army, Information Paper, *Army Stop Loss/Stop Movement Program*, March 11, 2004, "Soldiers normally not subject to the Army Stop Loss/Stop Movement Program[:] Those soldiers in violation of the Army's homosexual conduct policy." Tice, Jim, "Stop-Loss Extends to All on Active Duty," *Army Times*, February 25, 1991: 16. Those not covered by stop-loss include "soldiers eligible for disability retirement or separation, dependency, hardship, pregnancy, misconduct, punitive actions, unsatisfactory performance and homosexuality."

[29] U.S. Army, FORSCOM Mobilization and Deployment Planning System (FORMDEPS), FORSCOM Regulation 500-3-3, Volume III, Reserve Component Unit Commander's Handbook, Fort McPherson, Georgia, 15 July 1999: 27, 33.

[30] See Burrelli, David F., "An Overview of the Debate on Homosexuals in the U.S. Military," in *Gays and Lesbians in the Military, Issues, Concerns, and Contrasts,* Scott, Wilbur J., and Sandra Carson Stanley, eds., Aldine de Gruyter, New York, 1994: 18-19.

[31] Student's "t test," introduced by W.S. Gossett, under the pseudonym "Student," is used in this instance to measure differences of means between two sets of data taking into consideration the dispersion of data in each set and the number of cases involved in each set as well. These differences in means are considered in terms of their relative probability compared to random sampling distributions of samples of the same size. If the differences are small, as was the case here, the explanation that any difference is due to random factors in the data can not be rejected. In other words, the data do not support a conclusion that the change in policy had a statistical effect on discharge rates. See Blalock, Hubert M., Jr., *Social Statistics*, 2nd ed., New York: McGraw-Hill, 1972: 220-241. For these data, prob. t=1.3445 with 27 degrees of freedom.

[32] 478 U.S. 186 (1986) .

[33] Under the "policy" established by 10 U.S.C. §654 (b)(2), a service-member "shall be separated from the armed forces" where there is a finding:

That the member has stated that he or she is a homosexual or bisexual, or words to that effect, unless there is a further finding, made and approved in accordance with procedures set forth in the regulations, that the member has demonstrated that he or she is not a person who engages in, attempts to engage in, has a propensity to engage in, or intends to engage in homosexual acts.

[34] *Holmes v. California Army Nat'l Guard*, 525 U.S. 1067 (1999).

[35] 539 U.S. 558 (2003).

[36] Id. at 578.

[37] The Uniform Code of Military Justice, Article 125, provides for court-martial and punishment as the court-martial may direct, for acts of sodomy committed by military personnel.

[38] U.S. Const. art. I, § 8.

[39] *United States v. O'Brien*, 391 U.S. 367, 377 (1968).

[40] U.S. Const. art. II, § 2.

[41] *Goldman v. Weinberger*, 475 U.S. 503, 507 (1986).

[42] *Rostker v. Goldberg*, 453 U.S. 57 (1981).

[43] *Parker v. Levy*, 417 U.S. 733, 758 (1974).

[44] 475 U.S. 503 (1986); 453 U.S. 57 (1981).

[45] Id. at 507, quoting *Orloff v. Willoughby*, 345 U.S. 83, 92 (1953).

[46] Id. at 528 (O'Connor J., dissenting).

[47] 453 U.S. 57 (1981).

[48] 429 U.S. 190 (1976)

[49] Id. at 64-68.

[50] 80 F.3d 915 (4th Cir.), *cert. denied*, 519 U.S. 948 (1996).

[51] Id. at 931.

[52] 945 F. Supp. 924 (E.D.Va. 1996), aff'd per curiam, 139 F.3d 893 (4th Cir. 1998).

[53] 97 F.3d 256 (8th Cir. 1996), *cert. denied*, 522 U.S. 807 (U.S. 1997).

[54] 106 F.3d 1420 (9th Cir. 1997).

[55] *Holmes v. California Army Nat'l Guard; Watson v. Cohen*, 124 F.3d 1126 (9th Cir 1997), cert. denied, 525 U.S. 1067 (U.S. 1999).

[56] 124 F.3d at 1135. See also *Jackson v. Dep 't of the Air Force*, 132 F.3d 39 (9th Cir. 1997) (holding that homosexuals are not members of a suspect class, that the military's regulations are rationally related to a legitimate government interest, and are not arbitrary or irrational).

[57] 155 F.3d 628 (2d Cir. 1998).

[58] *Griswold v. Connecticut*, 381 U.S. 479 (1965).

[59] "Gay rights ruling gets test in military," *NLJ*, vol. 27, No. 7. pp 1, 33 (quoting David Cruz of the University of Southern California Law School).

[60] 60 M.J. 198 (C.A.A.F. 2004).

[61] Id. at 206-07.

[62] 68 Fed. Cl. 503 (Ct. Cl. 2005)

[63] Id. at 519. See also, United States v. Barrera, 2006 CCA LEXIS 215 (A.F. Ct. Crim. App. 2006).

[64] Army 2003 0534 (mem. op. November 30, 2004).

[65] But see United States v. Stephens, 2007 CCA LEXIS 428 (N-M.C.C.A. October 11, 2007).

[66] 527 F.3d 806 (9th Cir. 2008).

[67] Witt v. United States Dep't of the Air Force, 444 F. Supp. 2d 1138 (W.D. Wash. 2006).

[68] 527 F.3d 806, 817 (9th Cir. 2008).

[69] Sell v. United States, 539 U.S. 166 (U.S. 2003).

[70] 527 F.3d 806, 819 (9th Cir. 2008).

[71] 528 F.3d 42 (1st Cir. 2008).

[72] Id. at 52.

[73] Id. at 56.

[74] Id. at 60.

[75] The Winchell case is cited routinely in press reports, particularly when changes to the military's homosexual policy are considered. It is primarily for that reason that it is described here. Other cases have received considerably less attention. For instance, see

Jacobs, Sally, "Sexual Assault in the Shadows, Male victims in military cite devastating impact on career, life," *Boston Globe*, September 12, 2004: 1 or Price, Jay, "Guardsman Killed Iraqi After Sex," *Raleigh News & Observer*, December 18, 2004: 1.

[76] For a more thorough reading of the events surrounding Winchell's murder, see France, David, "An Inconvenient Woman," *The New York Times Magazine*, May 28, 2000: 24.

[77] "Although Army officials have not disclosed a motive for the attack—Winchell had gotten the best of the soldier in a fight a few days before the killing—local and national gay rights groups contend there is mounting evidence that Winchell was the victim of a hate crime." Pressley, Sue Anne, "Hate May Have Triggered Fatal Barracks Beating," *Washington Post*, August 11, 1999: 1.

[78] U.S. v Justin Fisher, affirmed, U.S. Court of Appeals for the Armed Forces, June 17, 2003, 58 M.J. 300(2003), Fisher's 14-year sentence was reduced as a result of a plea bargain; U.S. v. Glover, summarily affirmed, U.S. Court of Appeals for the Armed Forces, December 17, 2003, 59 M.J. 225(2003).

[79] Critics contend that gay rights advocates used the death of Winchell as a means of pursuing a larger agenda. "Even though cases of homosexual harassment in the military are few, a brutal murder at Fort Campbell following a 4th of July brawl has been cited as evidence of the need for anti-harassment sensitivity training." Donnelly, Elaine, "Activists keep pushing homosexual agenda for the armed forces," *Center for Military Readiness*, Issue no. 52, September 1999: 3.

[80] E.O. 13140, 1999 Amendments to the Manual for Courts-Martial, United States, sec. 1(d), 64 F.R. 55115, October 6, 1999.

[81] Crowley, Vince. "Anti-harassment Policy Stresses Respect," *The [Army] Times*, August 7, 2000: 24.

[82] This language was incorporated into various military training and other documents. These include the U.S. Army Basic Training Study Guide, *Dignity and Respect: A training guide on Homosexual Conduct Policy*, U.S. Army, 1 May 2001 and Army Regulation 350-1, Army Training and Education, 1-7(c)(1): "Treating soldiers with dignity and respect is an Army bedrock value. Soldiers will be treated with dignity and respect.... Harassment of soldiers for any reason, to include race, religion, national origin, sex, and perceived sexual orientation, will not be tolerated."

[83] Garamone, Jim, "Dignity, Respect at Heart of Anti-Harassment Plan," *Armed Forces Information Service*, July 21, 2000.

[84] Servicemembers Legal Defense Network, Conduct Unbecoming: The 10th Annual Report on "Don't Ask, Don't Tell, Don't Pursue, Don't Harass," 2004: 6, from an on-line press release.

[85] Crea, Joe, "Harassment Policy 'Not Necessary': Official," *The Washington Blade* at http://www.washblade.com/ 2004/7-30/news/national/pentagon.cfm.

[86] U.S. Department of Defense, Under Secretary of Defense (Personnel and Readiness), David S.C. Chu, Letter to The Honorable James Langevin, June 24, 2004.

[87] "Army Denies Kin's Claim in Killing of Private," *New York Times*, October 1, 2000, Associate Press, "Wrongful- Death Appeal Rejected," *Washington Times,* May 22, 2001: A8.

[88] Myers, Steven Lee, "Transfer of General at Site of Anti-Gay Killing is Protested," *New York Times*, June 9, 2000.

[89] McHugh, Jane, "Slain Soldier's Parents Fight General's Promotion," *Army Times*, May 26, 2003: 9; "A Controversial Appointment," *Army Times*, September 29, 2003: 4.

[90] Maze, Rick, "Robert Clark gets controversial third star," *Army Times*, December 1, 2003: 28.

[91] U.S. Congress. House, Conference Committee, Enactment of Provisions of H.R. 5408, The Floyd D. Spence National Defense Authorization Act for Fiscal Year 2001, 106th Cong., 2nd Sess., H.Rept. 106-945, October 6, 2000: 859; *Congressional Record*, October 8, 2004: H9561.

[92] This is not to be confused with earlier amendments offered by Rep. Solomon involving student assistance and compliance with Selective Service registration. As a result of these more

recent amendments, some have termed the first amendments "Solomon I" and the latter as "Solomon II." See Fraas, Charlotte, David Osman, Robert Goldich and David Ackerman, "Student Financial Aid and Draft Registration Compliance," CRS MB3213, Archived July 18, 1985.

[93] P.L. 97-252; 96 Stat. 748; September 8, 1982.

[94] This law was implemented under U.S., Department of Defense, Assistant Secretary of Defense, (MI&L), Directive 1304.24, *Use of Directory Information on Secondary School Students for Military Recruiting Purposes*, April 20, 1984.

[95] Mathews, Jay, "Oakland Bars Releasing Student Data to Military," *Washington Post,* January 18, 1991: A4.

[96] Two schools defy district ban on military recruiters, Associated Press, December 24, 1998.

[97] "Lift Ban On Military Recruiters," *Portland Oregonian*, July 24, 2000.

[98] P.L. 106-65; 113 Stat. 622; October 5, 1999.

[99] "Lift Ban On Military Recruiters," *Portland Oregonian*, July 24, 2000.

[100] P.L. 106-398; 114 Stat. 1654A-13 1; October 30, 2000. These changes were prompted by service complaints regarding the denial of access issue. "Approximately 2,000 public high schools have policies that bar military recruiters from one or more services, and high schools barred recruiters more than 19,000 times last year, according to a Pentagon spokeswoman." Easier Access For Military Recruiters, *Tampa Tribune*, July 6, 2000. Protesting the military's policy on homosexuals has been a common, but not the only explanation, offered in denying military access to campuses. For the purposes of this law, a "local educational agency" is defined under sec. 14 101(18) of the Elementary and Secondary Education Act of 1965 (20 United States Code 8801(18)).

[101] P.L. 107-107; 115 Stat. 1113; December 28, 2001.

[102] P.L. 107-110; 115 Stat. 1983; January 8, 2002. For more information, see CRS Report RS22362, *Military Recruitment Provisions Under the No Child Left Behind Act: A Legal Analysis*, by Jody Feder.

[103] Hayasaki, Erika, "Districts Taking On Recruiters," *Los Angeles Times*, February, 13, 2003; Hayasaki, Erika, "Campus Military Recruitment Roils Students," *Los Angeles Times*, February 8, 2004; and, Lewin, Tamar, "Uncle Sam Wants Student Lists, And Schools Fret," *New York Times*, January, 29, 2003.

[104] In 2003, the Department of Defense reported that the "total number of cadets in JROTC was 450,000 students in 3,050 schools worldwide." Leong, Brenda K., Major, OASD(P&R), letter to Susan Sanford, CRS, April 7, 2003.

[105] P.L. 108-136; 117 Stat. 1478; November 24, 2003.

[106] Liptak, Adam, "Defense Dept. Settles Suit On Database For Recruiting," *New York Times,* January 10, 2007: 19.

[107] Matthew B. Stannard, "Laws Restricting Recruiting Tossed," *San Francisco Chronicle*, June 19, 2009: B1; United States v. City of Arcata, 2009 U.S. Dist. LEXIS 57555 (N.D. Cal. June 17, 2009).

[108] Peterson, Bill, "Faculty Seeks ROTC's Ouster Over Policy on Gays," *Washington Post*, December 5, 1989: 14; Lewin, Tamar, "Harvard Protesting R.O.T.C. Rejection of Homosexuality," *New York Times*, June 15, 1990: 17; and, Behan, Catherine, "For gays, ROTC is one more battlefield," *Chicago Tribune*, May 9, 1991: 29. While some schools sought to have ROTC removed outright, at least one decided to cease awarding credit for ROTC classes. Matthews, William, "Colleges challenging DOD ban on homosexuals," *Air Force Times*, October 14, 1991: 18.

[109] Lewin, Tamar, "Navy Drops Efforts to seek Repayment From 2 Gay Students," *New York Times*, May 9, 1990: 19.

[110] See Hudson, Neff, "Gays ousted from ROTC get break," *Air Force Times*, June 27, 1994.

[111] P.L. 103-337; 108 Stat. 2776; October 5, 1994.

[112] P.L. 104-106, 110 Stat. 315; February 10, 1996.

[113] *Gay and Lesbian Law Students Association v. Board of Trustees*, 236 Conn. 453, 673 A.2d 484 (Conn. 1996). Judson, George, "Military Recruiting Ban On a Campus is Upheld," *New York Times*, March 20, 1996: B7.

[114] 12 Stat. 503; July 2, 1862.

[115] During the 1995-96 school year, a total of over 160 students participated in ROTC at UConn at Storrs, CT. The Air Force and Army have ROTC programs at UConn. UConn also sponsored those partaking in ROTC from Yale University since no such program is available at the Yale campus.

[116] P.L. 104-208, 110 Stat. 3009-270; September 30, 1996.

[117] *Congressional Record*, October 23, 1997: H9383; U.S. Department of Defense, "Military Recruiting and Reserve Officer Training Corps Access to Institutions of Higher Education," *Federal Register*, vol. 63, No. 205, October 23, 1998: 56819. The laws regarding campus access and ROTC were added to Title 10, USC, sec. 983 under P.L. 106-65; 113 Stat. 609; October 5, 1999.

[118] Compart, Andrew, "Connecticut returns recruiters to state colleges," *Army Times*, November 17, 1997: 6.

[119] P.L. 106-79; 113 Stat. 1260; October 25, 1999. In 2002, relating to the Coast Guard, this language was amended to substitute the Department of Homeland Security for the Department of Transportation. P.L. 107-296; 116 Stat. 2314; November 25, 2002.

[120] Morriss, Andrew, "Law Profs Throw SALT on 9/11 Wounds," *Wall Street Journal*, November 12, 2001.

[121] This may refer to Art. I, Section 8 of the Constitution.

[122] H.Con.Res. 36; Rep. Mike Rogers, February 1, 2005.

[123] 10 U.S.C. § 983(b)(1).

[124] Id. at § 983(c)(2).

[125] Id. at § 983(d)(1).

[126] Id. at § 983(d)(2).

[127] 126 S. Ct. 1297 (U.S. 2006).

[128] 530 U.S. 640 (2000).

[129] Brief for Respondents, at p. 36, Rumsfeld v. FAIR, No. 04-1152 (filed 9-21-2005).

[130] Id. at pp 11-13.

[131] U.S. Const., Art. I, § 8, Cls 1, 12 and 13.

[132] Brief for the Petitioners, at 2, Rumsfeld v. FAIR, No. 04-1152 (filed July 2005).

[133] Id. at 19.

[134] Rumsfeld v. Forum for Academic & Inst. Rights, Inc., 126 S. Ct. 1297, 1308 (2006) (citing *West Virginia Bd. of Ed. v. Barnette*, 319 U.S. 624, 642 (1943)(voiding state law requiring school children to recite Pledge of Allegiance and to salute the flag); *Wooley v. Maynard*, 430 U.S. 705, 717 (1977)(holding unconstitutional New Hampshire law requiring state motorist to display state motto—"Live Free or Die"—on their license plates).

[135] Id. at 1309.

[136] Id. at 1310.

[137] 530 U.S. 640 (2000).

[138] Forum for Academic & Inst. Rights, Inc., 126 S. Ct. at 1312.

[139] Id. at 1311.

[140] CRS Report RL3 1994, *Same-Sex Marriages: Legal Issues*, by Alison M. Smith.

[141] P.L. 104-199; 110 Stat. 2419; September 21, 1996.

[142] Summerskill, Ben, "Brits' Lifting Of Military Ban On Gays Not Found To Hurt Morale," *San Diego Union-Tribune*, December 25, 2000.

[143] Branigin, William, "Australian Military Adjusting To Policy Allowing Gay Troops," *Washington Post*, March 30, 1993: 6.

[144] "Army Welcomes Gays," *Moscow Times*, November 8, 2003: 4.

[145] U.S. Congress. Senate. Committee on Armed Services, Hearings, Policy Concerning Homosexuality in the Armed Forces, Comments by Prof. Charles Moskos, Senate Hearings 103-845, 103rd Cong., 2nd Sess., 1994: 352.

CHAPTER SOURCES

The following chapters have been previously published:

Chapter 1 – This is an edited, excerpted and augmented edition of a United States Congressional Research Service publication, Report Order Code RS21897, dated January 3, 2008.

Chapter 2 – This is an edited, excerpted and augmented edition of a United States Congressional Research Service publication, Report Order Code RS21191, dated February 2, 2009.

Chapter 3 – This is an edited, excerpted and augmented edition of a United States Congressional Research Service publication, Report Order Code RL31994, dated June 9, 2009.

Chapter 4 – This is an edited, excerpted and augmented edition of a United States Congressional Research Service publication, Report Order Code RL30113, dated July 22, 2009.

INDEX

D

H

I

J

K

L

R

S

T

U

V